# *The Dallas Cowboys Wives'*
# COOKBOOK

Compiled by The Dallas Cowboys' Wives

Happy Hill Farm Academy/Home
Star Route, Box 56
Granbury, Texas 76048

Copyright 1992

# HAPPY HILL FARM ACADEMY/HOME
Star Route, Box 56
Granbury, Texas 76048

## SECOND EDITION

First Printing: 10,000 copies, October, 1992

Other Dallas Cowboys Wives' Books:

DALLAS COWBOYS WIVES' COOKBOOK
(FIRST EDITION) 1991
First Printing: 10,000 copies, November, 1991

Printed in the United States of America
Printed by
BRANCH-SMITH
Fort Worth, Texas

All of the proceeds from the sale of this cookbook go directly to the Scholarship Fund at Happy Hill Farm Academy/Home, supporting deserving boys and girls (ages 5-18), who live, work, and study on the 500-acre working-farm campus located just outside the Dallas-Fort Worth Metroplex. The Farm is licensed by the Texas Department of Human Services as a residential treatment center, but does not receive State or Federal funding.

# ACKNOWLEDGEMENTS

As the popularity of a new generation of Dallas Cowboys grows, so does fan interest. The folks who follow the Cowboys faithfully want to know what goes on behind-the-scenes -- inside information about the players, coaches, their wives and families -- even what they like to eat!

Last year's "Dallas Cowboys Wives' Cookbook" was gathered up with such enthusiasm that the players' and coaches' wives have teamed up to do it again this year. They've just released the all-new "Dallas Cowboys Wives' Cookbook - Edition II".

This year's cookbook features regional Dallas Cowboys' favorite recipes (from the North, South, East, and West). All of the pictures of the players, coaches, wives, and families are different from last year's cookbook, as well as the biographical section, which has also been expanded to include interesting information about the Dallas Cowboys that is not found in other publications.

The Cookbook Committee was headed by Gina Gesek, but wives, players, and coaches had a part in the production of the book. Charlotte Anderson, Special Events Coordinator for the Dallas Cowboys, and her staff, threw their energies into the project to make this cookbook one that every Cowboys fan and cookbook lover will want to have.

The cover photography, along with other photos used in marketing and promotion, were donated by Dave Edmunson of Edmunson and Father - Dallas, Texas.

Design concepts and art for both the cookbook and marketing materials were produced by Mosaic Creative, Inc., with special thanks to Stan Tuzent and Martin Massinger.

## ACKNOWLEDGEMENTS (continued)

Gloria, my wife, and Todd Shipman, our son, set type, read proof, and did all the things necessary for production.

Russ Russell and Jim Browder, of the "Dallas Cowboy Weekly," have been especially helpful in allowing us to use "Weekly" pictures as necessary to supplement those provided by the players' families.

The members of the Jones' family and the Dallas Cowboys organization have graciously cooperated by supplying us with information and allowing us the use of the Cowboy logo. To the many new friends we have made throughout the front office, we are grateful. Your assistance and encouragement were invaluable.

A special word of appreciation to John and Gina Gesek, who again headed the cookbook project. They encouraged others to help, wrote letters, made telephone calls, made personal appearances, and much more. Such an undertaking requires lots of time -- time that John and Gina could have spent with their family and friends. To you, we owe a debt of gratitude.

To everyone who had a part in "Edition II" -- God bless you!

C. Edward Shipman
Executive Director
HAPPY HILL FARM ACADEMY/HOME

_Dallas Cowboys Wives' Cookbook_

# DALLAS COWBOYS

# 1992

## PRESIDENT - GENERAL MANAGER'S (WIFE)

Mrs. Jerry Jones (Gene)

## HEAD COACH

Jimmy Johnson

## PLAYERS' WIVES

Mrs. Tommy Agee (Anchylus)
Mrs. Bill Bates (Denise)
Mrs. Tony Casillas (Lisa)
Mrs. Dixon Edwards (Secola)
Mrs. Kenneth Gant (Aris)
Mrs. John Gesek (Gina)
Mrs. Kevin Gogan (Heather)
Mrs. Alvin Harper (Jamise)
Mrs. Dale Hellestrae (Brooke)
Mrs. Issiac Holt (Burnedean)
Mrs. Ray Horton (Leslie)
Mrs. Michael Irvin (Sandy)
Mrs. Jim Jeffcoat (Tammy)
Mrs. Kelvin Martin (Lynn)
Mrs. Nate Newton (Dorothy)
Mrs. Ken Norton, Jr. (Angela)
Mrs. Jay Novacek (Yvette)
Mrs. Alfredo Roberts (Angel)
Mrs. Mike Saxon (Sherri)
Mrs. Mark Tuinei (Pono)
Mrs. James Washington (Dana)

v

# DALLAS COWBOYS

# 1992

## SINGLE PLAYERS

Troy Aikman
Steve Beuerlein
Larry Brown
Tony Hill
Daryl Johnston
Jimmie Jones
Leon Lett
Russell Maryland
Godfrey Myles
Emmitt Smith
Vinson Smith
Mark Stepnoski
Tony Tolbert
Alan Veingrad
Erik Williams
Robert Williams

## ROOKIES' & RECENTLY-ACQUIRED PLAYERS' WIVES

Mrs. Frank Cornish (Robin)
Mrs. Melvin Evans (Edith Renee)
Mrs. Melvin Foster (Stacy)
Mrs. Chad Hennings (Tammy)
Mrs. Robert Jones (Maneesha)

# DALLAS COWBOYS

# 1991

## SINGLE ROOKIES & RECENTLY-ACQUIRED PLAYERS

Michael Beasley
Greg Briggs
Tim Daniel
Lin Elliott
Patt Evans
Jason Garrett
Clayton Holmes
Todd Jones
Jimmy Smith
Kevin Smith
Fallon Wacasey
Darren Woodson

## COACHING STAFF'S WIVES

Mrs. Hubbard Alexander (Gloria)
Mrs. Neill Armstrong (Jane)
Mrs. Joe Avezzano (Diann)
Mrs. Robert Blackwell (Dana)
Mrs. Joe Brodsky (Joyce)
Mrs. Buck Buchanan (Geraldine)
Mrs. Dave Campo (Kay)
Mrs. Don Cochren (Jan)
Mrs. Butch Davis (Tammy)
Mrs. Robert Ford (Janice)
Mrs. Steve Hoffman (Raffy)
Mrs. Jim Maurer (Rosanne)

*Dallas Cowboys Wives' Cookbook*

# DALLAS COWBOYS

# 1991

## COACHING STAFF'S WIVES
(continued)

Mrs. Bruce Mays (Kathy)
Mrs. Kevin O'Neill (Anne)
Mrs. Bob Slowik (Carol)
Mrs. Norv Turner (Nancy)
Mrs. Dave Wannstedt (Jan)

## SINGLE COACHES

Tony Wise
Mike Woicik

# FOREWORD

As the economic crisis in our state and nation continues, organizations like HAPPY HILL FARM ACADEMY/HOME are being asked to assume an even greater role in providing for the needs of the at-risk children and their families. The importance of volunteerism is without measure. The efforts of the Dallas Cowboys' Wives in behalf of the children of HAPPY HILL FARM is an example of volunteerism at its best. HAPPY HILL FARM ACADEMY/HOME, in its eighteenth year of existence, has neither sought nor received any Federal or State aid. All of its support comes from individuals, foundations, corporations, and churches. All of the proceeds from the sale of this book go directly to the Scholarship Fund to underwrite the care of indigent children who live, work, and study at HAPPY HILL FARM. Neither the Cowboys' Wives, nor anyone in the Dallas Cowboy organization, receive any funds from this effort.

HAPPY HILL FARM ACADEMY/HOME is located just outside the Dallas-Fort Worth Metroplex. On its 500-acre working-farm campus live boys and girls whose personal problems have made it impossible for them to live in traditional home or school settings. The Farm is licensed as a residential treatment facility by the Texas Department of Human Services. Inter-denominational in nature, strong moral and spiritual teachings undergird the work. In its own fully-accredited (Southern Association of Colleges and Schools) private school (K-12 grades), the Farm's children are taught the merits of the free-enterprise system and the importance of hard work. A Board of Directors, including Bob Breunig -- former Dallas Cowboy middle linebacker, assists the Executive Director in the operation of the Farm.

Many caring, sharing supporters make the ministry of Happy Hill Farm possible. If you would like to know more about how you can become involved in the lives of troubled, needy boys and girls, please write or call for information.

## HAPPY HILL FARM
### Star Route, Box 56
### Granbury, Texas 76048

### Phone: (817) 897-4822

# TABLE OF CONTENTS

Page

xi

Page

|  | Page |
|---|---|
| **FRANK & ROBIN CORNISH** | 170 |
| Frank's Southern Chocolate Pound Cake | 172 |
| Jeanette's Seafood Casserole | 172 |
| | |
| **TIM DANIEL** | 173 |
| Tim's Old South Barbecued Chicken | 174 |
| Daniel's Blueberry-Oatmeal Bread | 174 |
| | |
| **LIN ELLIOTT** | 175 |
| Lin's Chicken Spaghetti | 176 |
| Elliott's Butter Sugar Cookies | 176 |
| | |
| **MELVIN & EDITH RENEE EVANS** | 178 |
| Melvin Evans' Old-Fashioned Pound Cake | 180 |
| Edith Renee's Fruit Cottage Cheese Salad | 180 |
| | |
| **PATT EVANS** | 181 |
| Patt's Pasta Primavera | 182 |
| Evans' Hot Sausage Sandwiches | 182 |
| Patt Evans' Crunchy Jumbles | 182 |
| | |
| **MELVIN & STACY FOSTER** | 184 |
| Melvin's Mom's Enchilada Casserole | 186 |
| Stacy's Buster Bar Dessert | 186 |
| | |
| **JASON GARRETT** | 187 |
| Garrett's Oriental Shrimp | 188 |
| Jason's Linguine and Creamy White Clam Sauce | 188 |
| Jason Garrett's Fruit Shake | 188 |
| | |
| **CHAD & TAMMY HENNINGS** | 190 |
| Chad's Country Ribs | 192 |
| Tammy's Chicken and Sour Cream Enchiladas | 192 |
| | |
| **CLAYTON HOLMES** | 193 |
| Hershey-Chocolate Cake with Cream Cheese Icing | 194 |
| Clayton Holmes' Broccoli Casserole | 194 |

xv

# ADMINISTRATION

## GENE & JERRAL (JERRY) WAYNE JONES
### President and General Manager
### Dallas Cowboys Football Club

**BIRTHDATES:** *Jerry* – 10-13-42 (Inglewood, California); *Gene* – 2-14-42 (Little Rock, Arkansas)

**COLLEGES:** *Jerry* – University of Arkansas (Masters – Business Administration); *Gene* – University of Arkansas (Liberal Arts)

**GREATEST MOMENT IN SPORTS:** Coaching Sons' Little League Teams

**WIFE'S OCCUPATION:** Mother and Grandmother

**HONORS OR AWARDS:** *Jerry* – Starred in Football as a Running Back at North Little Rock High School, Receiving a Scholarship to Play at the University of Arkansas; Starting Guard and Co-Captain of the 1964 National Championship Razorback Football Team (11-0); Boys Club Award; Awarded the Big "D" Award by the DASA; Edelstein Pro Football Letter NFL Owner of the Year; *Gene* – 1992 Arkansas Woman of Distinction; TACA Executive Board; Board Member of Children's Medical Center of Dallas; Mental Health Center; Willis M. Tate Distinguished Lecture Series; Easter Seals; Member of Symphony and Dallas Museum of Art

**HOBBIES & INTERESTS:** *Jerry* – Hunting, Snow Skiing, and Playing Tennis with His Children; His New Granddaughter; Involved in Numerous Civic and Charitable Causes; *Gene* – Children and First Grandchild; Snow Skiing, Walking the Beach, Traveling, Football, and Civic and Charitable Activities

**FAVORITE AUTHOR:** *Jerry* – Tom Clancy; *Gene* – John Grisham

**FAVORITE TYPE OF MUSIC:** *Jerry* – Country Western; *Gene* – Scores from Broadway Musicals

**FAVORITE SPORTS HERO:** *Jerry* – Vince Lombardi; *Gene* – Husband Jerry

**FAVORITE TV/MOVIE STAR:** *Jerry* – Sean Connery; *Gene* – Robert Redford and Paul Newman

**FAVORITE FOOD:** *Jerry* – Popcorn; *Gene* – Cookies

**CHILDREN & AGES:** Stephen - 28 yrs. (Wife: Karen; and Daughter: Jessica); Charlotte - 26 yrs. (Husband: Shy Anderson); and Jerry, Jr. - 23 yrs.

## JERRY'S TEXAS NIBBLERS

2 boxes thin pretzels    1 box croutons (onion and garlic)
1 box Rice Chex    2 cans mixed nuts
1 box Corn Chex    1 pkg. whole pecans
1 box Cheerios    2 pkg. Cheddar cheese fish crackers
     (Pepperidge Farms)

Mix together the above ingredients.

*Sauce:* 7-1/2 sticks margarine    3 t. garlic powder
1-1/2 c. Crisco Oil    3 t. allspice powder
6 T. Worcestershire sauce    dash of red pepper
2-1/2 T. Accent seasoning    dash of pepper sauce

Prepare sauce. Heat to boiling; pour over dry ingredients. Mix carefully, always stirring from the bottom. Put in shallow pans. Bake at 200 degrees for 3-4 hours. Stir often to coat evenly. Makes a popcorn can almost full.

## GENE'S BROCCOLI AND RICE CASSEROLE

1 medium onion, chopped    1/2 lb. Velveeta cheese
3 t. margarine    3 c. cooked rice
1 c. cream of chicken soup    1 pkg. broccoli, chopped
1/2 c. milk

Saute onions in margarine; add cream of chicken soup. Heat and fold in cooked rice. Add chopped broccoli, which has been thawed enough to break into pieces. Pour into greased casserole dish (9" x 13"). Cover top with cheese. Cover; bake at 350 degrees for 30 minutes. *Option: Boil 2 c. diced chicken until tender. Remove chicken from broth. Cook rice in broth; add to above ingredients.*

4

## JERRY JONES' POTATO CASSEROLE

2 lbs. frozen hash brown potatoes
1/2 c. butter, melted
1 t. salt
1/2 t. pepper
2 T. onions, minced
1/2 c. milk
1 can cream of chicken soup
1 pt. sour cream
2 c. American cheese, grated
1/4 c. butter
2 c. corn flakes, crushed

Place the frozen hash brown potatoes in the bottom of a pan (9" x 13"). Combine butter, salt, pepper, minced onion, milk, cream of chicken soup, and sour cream; pour mixture over potatoes. Top with cheese. Combine butter and crushed corn flakes; sprinkle on top of cheese. Bake at 375 degrees for 40 minutes.

## JERRY'S AND GENE'S CHILI STUFF

2 lbs. ground chuck
1 bottle Kraft Thick & Spicy Barbeque Sauce
1 onion, chopped
1 bell pepper, chopped
1 large can Campbell's Pork & Beans

Brown meat; pour off grease. Combine remaining ingredients; pour over meat. Simmer for one hour.

5

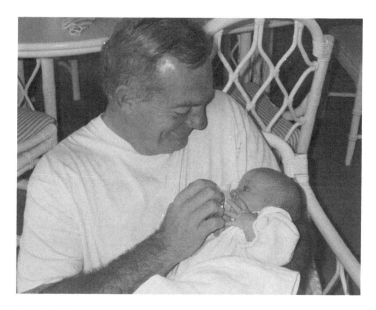

Jerry holding Jessica Jones, his first grandchild

Charlotte Jones Anderson, the Marketing and Special Events Coordinator for the Cowboys, and her husband, Shy Anderson

Jerry Jones, Jr., a recent graduate of Georgetown University, and his mother, Gene Jones, a former Arkansas beauty pageant winner

Karen, Jessica, and Stephen Jones, who is a vice president of the Dallas Cowboys Football Club

## JAMES (JIMMY) WILLIAM JOHNSON
### Head Coach
### Dallas Cowboys Football Club

**BIRTHDATE:** 7-16-43 (Port Arthur, Texas)

**COLLEGE:** University of Arkansas (Psychology)

**HONORS OR AWARDS:** Earned All-State Football Honors at Jefferson High School in Port Arthur as a Two-Way Lineman; Became an All-Southwest Conference Defensive Lineman at Arkansas; Three-Year Letterman, Named to Arkansas' All-Decade Team of the 1960's; at Oklahoma State -- Named Big Eight Coach of the Year Following His First Season; at the University of Miami (1984-1988) -- Led Hurricanes to a 52-9 Record, Including a 44-4 Mark over the Final Four Seasons; His Hurricane Teams Captured Two Orange Bowl Titles, National Championship in 1987, and Two No. 2 Finishes (1986 and 1988); Named by Jerry Jones as the Dallas Cowboys Head Coach on February 25, 1989; Visibly Characterized by One Sharply-Focused Purpose -- That of Constantly Improving the Football Team; in 1990, Named NFL Coach of the Year by the Associated Press, and NFC Coach of the Year by United Press International and College & Pro Football Newsweekly; 1991 -- Brought the Cowboys to an 11-5 Record, the Club's Best Record since 1983; Brought the Cowboys to a 1991 Playoff Victory in Chicago, Marking the Team's First Post Season Win since 1982 -- Also the Cowboys' First Road Playoff Victory since the 1980 Season; in the Last Two Seasons, Coached Dallas to Claim One Victory over 10 of the 12 NFC Teams that the Team Has Faced; in 1991, Named NFL Coach of the Year by Football Digest

**CHILDREN & AGES:** Brent, an attorney - 28 yrs.; and Chad, an account executive - 26 yrs.

8

## JIMMY JOHNSON'S SEAFOOD GUMBO

1 lb. fresh jumbo shrimp, with heads
carcasses, or heads, of 2 fish (3-5 lb.)
1 medium onion, quartered
1 stalk celery, quartered
1 medium tomato, peeled and quartered
2 qts. water
3 T. gumbo file
1 t. salt                             2 c. onion, coarsely-chopped
1/2 t. white pepper                   2 c. celery, coarsely-chopped
1/2 t. black pepper                   2 c. green pepper, coarsely-
1/2 t. ground red pepper                 chopped
1-1/2 t. Hungarian paprika            1 T. hot sauce
1 t. garlic, minced                   1 can tomato sauce with tomato
1/2 t. dried whole thyme                 bits (15-oz.)
1/2 t. dried whole oregano            1 doz. fresh oysters, shucked
1 bay leaf, crushed                   1-1/2 c. flaked crab meat
3/4 c. butter or margarine            hot cooked rice

Remove shrimp heads and shells, reserving both. Devein shrimp; set aside in refrigerator. Combine shrimp heads and shells, fish carcasses, and next 4 ingredients in a 6-qt. Dutch oven; bring to a boil. Reduce heat and simmer (uncovered) for 6-8 hours. (*Add water as necessary to maintain 2 qts.*) Strain stock through cheesecloth, discarding solids; set stock aside. Combine next 10 ingredients; set aside. Melt butter in a 4-qt. Dutch oven over medium heat; stir in next 4 ingredients and seasoning mixture. Increase heat to high; cook for 6 minutes, stirring constantly. Add tomato sauce; cook over medium heat for 5 minutes, stirring constantly and scraping bottom. Stir in seafood stock; bring to a boil. Reduce heat; simmer (uncovered) for 45 minutes to 1 hour, stirring occasionally. Stir in shrimp, oysters, and crab meat; cover and turn off heat. Let stand 6-10 minutes, or until edges of oysters curl and shrimp are pink. Serve over rice. Makes about 2 quarts.

Johnson has made the Cowboys winners sooner than expected -- rapid success has been a trademark of his coaching career

Coach Jimmy Johnson with two sons (*picture taken by David Woo, photographer, at the "Dallas Morning News")

# VETERANS

## ANCHYLUS & THOMAS LEE (TOMMIE) AGEE
## *Number 34*
## Fullback -- 6-0 -- 225

**BIRTHDATES:** *Tommie* -- 2-22-64 (Maplesville, Alabama); *Anchylus* -- 6-18-62 (Union Springs, Alabama)

**COLLEGES:** *Tommie* -- Auburn University (B.S. -- Criminal Justice); *Anchylus* -- Troy State University (B.S. -- Business Administration)

**GREATEST MOMENT IN SPORTS:** Winning the Southeastern Conference Championship Game in College

**GREATEST THRILL ABOUT BEING A PRO ATHLETE:** Being in a Position to be a Positive Role Model for Youth

**FAVORITE ACADEMIC SUBJECT:** *Tommie* -- History; *Anchylus* -- Math (Accounting)

**WIFE'S OCCUPATION:** Full-time Mother

**HONORS OR AWARDS:** *Tommie* -- All-State Honors in Football, Basketball, and Track; Special Teams Captain at Auburn; *Anchylus* -- "Who's Who among American High School Students;" Received the George C. Wallace Academic Scholarship for Valedictorian's among High School Students

**HOBBIES & INTERESTS:** *Tommie* -- Hunting, Fishing, and Horseback Riding; Speaker for the Fellowship of Christian Athletes; Anti-Drug Campaign Speaker for Youth; Youth Counselor for the Alabama Department of Youth Services; *Anchylus* -- Loves Sports; Interested in Social Issues Concerning Our Society's Youth

**FAVORITE AUTHOR:** *Tommie* -- Alex Haley

**FAVORITE TYPE OF MUSIC:** *Tommie* -- All Types; *Anchylus* -- Blues and Jazz

**FAVORITE SPORTS HERO:** *Tommie* -- William Andrews; *Anchylus* -- Husband Tommie

**FAVORITE TV/MOVIE STAR:** *Tommie* -- Bill Cosby; *Anchylus* -- Wesley Snipes

**FAVORITE FOOD:** *Tommie* -- Grandma's Pork Chop Casserole; *Anchylus* -- Potato Dishes

**CHILDREN & AGES:** Tyler Walker -- Born 8-30-92

## TOMMIE'S GRILLED LEMON CHICKEN

2 chickens, quartered
lemon juice (from 3 lemons)
2 T. vegetable oil
1 T. salt
1 T. ground pepper
2-1/2 T. celery salt
1/4 t. red pepper

Place the quartered chicken pieces in a pan. Pour lemon juice over the chicken; chill for approximately 2 hours. Remove chicken from the juice; rub with vegetable oil. Combine all other ingredients; sprinkle over the chicken. Put on a grill (skin side up); cook until done.

## ANCHYLUS' SWEET POTATO PIE

2 medium-size potatoes
1 c. Carnation Milk
1 c. sugar
1/2 c. margarine
1 t. vanilla
1 t. flour
1/2 t. nutmeg
1 ready-made pie crust

Boil the potatoes until done; place in a mixing bowl. Add the other ingredients; blend well. Pour into the pie crust. Bake at 325 degrees until done.

Tommie is a capable blocker, runner, and receiver out of the backfield, and an outstanding contributor to the special teams units

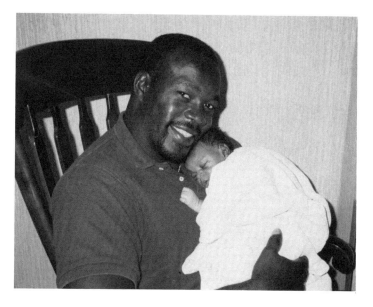

Tommie Agee with son, Tyler Walker -- born August 30, 1992

Anchylus and Tommie are both from Alabama

## TROY KENNETH AIKMAN
*\* Number 8 \**
Quarterback -- 6-4 -- 222

**BIRTHDATE:** 11-21-66 -- West Covina, California

**COLLEGE:** U.C.L.A. (Sociology)

**FAVORITE ACADEMIC SUBJECT:** Math

**GREATEST MOMENT IN SPORTS:** Being Named to the 1991 Pro Bowl

**GREATEST THRILL ABOUT BEING A PRO ATHLETE:** The Ability to Help People (Especially Children) Who Are Less Fortunate Than We Are

**YEARS IN PROFESSIONAL FOOTBALL:** 4th Season

**HONORS OR AWARDS:** Earned All-State Honors at Henryetta High School in Oklahoma; Town of Henryetta Named a Street after Aikman; an All-American, Finished His Collegiate Career as the Third Rated Passer in NCAA History; Named to Most All-Rookie Teams; in 1990, Named to the All-Madden Team; in 1991, Named to the Pro Bowl; in 1992, One of the Five Finalists for the NFL Man of the Year

**HOBBIES & INTERESTS:** Sponsors a Scholarship at His Former High School for Students Who Want to Attend College But Can't Afford It; Set up a Permanently-Endowed Scholarship at U.C.L.A.; Established The Troy Aikman Foundation to Benefit Children's Charities

**FAVORITE FOOD:** Italian

**FAVORITE TYPE OF MUSIC:** Country

**FAVORITE SPORTS HERO:** Larry Bird

**FAVORITE TV/MOVIE STAR:** Toss-Up between Tom Whitenight ("Necessary Roughness") and Michael Douglas

**PET PEEVE:** "Anything That Tests My Patience (or Lack of)"

**WORST FEAR:** Failure

## AIKMAN'S BLACK BUCK TRAIL DRIVE STYLE
*This recipe comes from Executive Chef John Billings at the
Y. O. Ranch Hilton in Kerrville, Texas.*

8 Black Buck medallions (2-oz. -- preferably back strap)
1/2 c. mushrooms, sliced
1/4 c. tomatoes, diced
1/2 c. red onion, julienne
1 T. fresh garlic, chopped
1 T. cilantro, chopped
1/8 c. jalapeno, chopped

2 oz. olive oil
1/2 c. red wine
1/2 c. white wine
1/4 c. water
salt and pepper, to taste

Sprinkle medallions with salt, pepper, and garlic. Pound Black Buck medallions with meat hammer until about 1/4" to 1/2" thick. Place saute pan on burner; put in olive oil -- get it hot. Place medallions in pan and sear one side; turn over and sear other side. Add mushrooms, tomatoes, onion, garlic, jalapeno, and cilantro. Continue cooking until meat reaches desired doneness. Remove meat from pan; place on warm platter. Drain grease. Place pan with veggies back on burner. Glaze pan with white and red wine. Add water. Add salt, to taste. Prepare *Roux*; add to pan to thicken juices to a medium consistency. Pour over the meat and serve. Serves 4 people.

*Roux*: Mix to form a paste (*roux*): 1/2 c. butter, melted
3/4 c. flour

## TROY'S CHOCOLATE-CHERRY CAKE

1 pkg. chocolate fudge cake mix
1 can cherry pie filling (21-oz.)

1 t. almond extract
2 eggs, beaten

Heat oven to 350 degrees. Using solid shortening, grease 9" x 13" pan. In bowl, combine first four ingredients by hand; stir until well-blended. Pour in pan; bake 25-30 minutes, or until it tests done. When cake comes out of oven, begin making the frosting.

*Frosting*: 1 c. sugar
5 T. margarine
1/3 c. milk

chocolate chips, semi-sweet (6-oz. pkg.)

In small saucepan, combine sugar, butter, and milk. Boil, stirring constantly, for 2 minutes. Remove from heat; stir in chocolate chips until smooth. Immediately pour over partially-cooled cake.

In two seasons at U.C.L.A., Aikman completed 64.8 percent of his passes for 5,298 yards and 41 touchdowns

Troy, in uniform with the Irving Police Department, is very interested in helping people -- especially children

Troy Aikman with his Black Buck Antelope in February, 1992

# DENISE & WILLIAM FREDERICK (BILL) BATES
## * *Number 40* *
### Safety -- 6-1 -- 203

BIRTHDATES: *Bill* -- 6-6-61 (Knoxville, Tennessee); *Denise* -- 1-25-60 (Nashville, Tennessee)

COLLEGES: *Bill* -- University of Tennessee (Economics); *Denise* -- University of Tennessee (B.A. -- Interior Design)

WIFE'S OCCUPATION: Mother; Co-Owner / Operator of Bill Bates Cowboy Ranch in McKinney, Texas

HONORS OR AWARDS: *Bill* -- Named Second-Team All-Southeastern Conference in Junior and Senior Seasons in College; Captain of College Team; NFL Alumni Special Teams Player of the Year in 1983 and 1984; Pro Bowl in 1985; 1985 NFL Man of the Year Finalist; All-Madden Teams in 1987, 1988, and 1990; Bob Lilly Award in 1990; Special Teams Captain in 1991

HOBBIES & INTERESTS: *Bill* -- Golf, Music, Fishing, Snow Skiing, and Horseback Riding; *Denise* -- Painting Children's Clothing to Sell in Craft Booth

FAVORITE AUTHOR; *Bill* -- Tom Clancy; *Denise* -- Sidney Sheldon

FAVORITE TYPE OF MUSIC: *Bill* -- Rock and Country; *Denise* -- Soft Rock

FAVORITE SPORTS HERO: *Bill* -- Dick Butkus and Bart Starr; *Denise* -- Husband Bill

FAVORITE TV/MOVIE STAR: *Bill* -- Mel Gibson; *Denise* -- Jeanene Turner ("Northern Exposure")

FAVORITE FOOD: *Bill* -- Fajitas; *Denise* -- Italian

CHILDREN & AGES: (Triplets) Graham, Brianna, and Hunter - 3-1/2 yrs.; Tanner - 1-1/2 yrs.

## BILL'S TENNESSEE PULLED-PORK BARBEQUE

1 pork shoulder (6-8 lbs.)

*Sauce:*        2 c. ketchup
            1 c. brown sugar
            1/4 c. vinegar
            2 T. yellow prepared mustard
            1 T. Worcestershire sauce
            1 t. lemon juice
            salt and pepper, to taste

Place pork shoulder in a large Dutch oven; cover with foil. Bake in oven at 275 degrees all night, or at least 8 hours. Remove from oven; let cool enough to touch. Pull meat from bone with fingers; "string" the larger pieces, discarding the fat. Place meat in a large casserole dish or Dutch oven; prepare sauce. Combine all ingredients in a saucepan; bring to a boil and simmer for 10 minutes. Pour sauce over meat; cover with foil. Place back in oven; bake at 275 degrees for 3 hours. (*Serve on warmed hamburger buns with your favorite trimmings!*)


## DENISE'S PEACH CRISP

4 c. sliced peaches (or other fruit)
1-1/2 c. sugar
3/4 c. brown sugar
1/2 c. flour
1 t. cinnamon
6 T. butter
3/4 c. oatmeal

Butter the bottom of a 2-qt. casserole dish. Toss fruit with sugar; place in bottom of dish. Make crumb topping by cutting the butter with the remaining ingredients; sprinkle on top of fruit. Bake at 375 degrees for 25-30 minutes, or until bubbly. Serve with ice cream while still warm.

Denise, Bill, and the children can still all fit in Dad's locker

The Bates' triplets: Graham William, Brianna Gail, and Hunter James -- accompanied by little brother, Tanner Forest

Winner of the Bob Lilly Award in each of the past two seasons, Bill Bates displays leadership and character on and off the field

# STEVE BEUERLEIN
## * Number 7 *
### Quarterback -- 6-2 -- 213

**BIRTHDATE:** 3-7-65 -- Los Angeles, California

**COLLEGE:** Notre Dame (B.A. -- Communications; Minor in Business)

**GREATEST MOMENT IN SPORTS:** Finishing the Win over the Washington Redskins Last Year and Quarterbacking into the Playoffs

**GREATEST THRILL ABOUT BEING A PRO ATHLETE:** The Opportunities That Are Extended to Us in So Many Different Areas -- Especially the Opportunity to Influence and Impact Kids; and the Thrill to be Living out a Childhood Dream

**HONORS OR AWARDS:** Two-Year Letterman in Football at Servite High School in Anaheim; Earned All-America Recognition from Scholastic Coach Magazine; as a Senior, Named the Orange County Player of the Year, after Leading His School to the No. 1 Ranking in the State; Stand-Out Performer in Basketball, Baseball, and as a Diver on the Swimming Team; Received Honorable Mention All-America by Associated Press

**HOBBIES & INTERESTS:** Golf and Reading

**FAVORITE ACADEMIC SUBJECT:** Spanish (Used to Be Fairly Fluent!)

**FAVORITE FOOD:** Mexican

**FAVORITE TYPE OF MUSIC:** Rock 'n Roll and Progressive

**FAVORITE SPORTS HERO:** Terry Bradshaw and Bert Jones

**FAVORITE TV/MOVIE STAR:** Steve Martin

**WORST FEAR:** "Spiders . . . and Texas Has Lots of 'Em!"

26

## STEVE BEUERLEIN'S CAJUN SEAFOOD FEAST

miniature corn cobs
new potatoes
Cajun seasoning (your choice)
fresh crab (King or Snow, or both)
clams, mussels, crawfish, shrimp, white fish -- all fresh (cut-up into bite-size pieces)
butter (lots!)

*Amounts of each ingredient vary with the amount of people to be served.*

Bring *large* pot of water to a boil. Add miniature corn cobs and new potatoes, along with Cajun seasoning (as much as you want). Let boil for 6-8 minutes. Add *everything else*, in any order, as much as you want. Let boil for 6-8 minutes (or until you think it's ready). When done, pour out water; strain everything. Cover a table with newspapers -- just pile it all on the table.

*No silverware necessary! Just grab what you want, dip into melted butter, and chow down!*

## BEUERLEIN'S TACO SALAD

ground beef                    lettuce, broken into pieces
Cheddar cheese, grated         tomato, cut in chunks
tortilla chips (plain Tostitos, broken into pieces)

Brown ground beef. Add other ingredients; mix well.

*Sauce*: Catalina Dressing, combined with Picante Sauce (Pace) or Taco Sauce

Pour sauce over the mixture of other ingredients.

*Amount of ingredients varies, dependent upon appetite!*

Steve is involved in several charitable activities in the off-season, including active roles with children's charities

Beuerlein quarterbacked the team in relief of the injured Aikman, guiding Dallas to four straight wins in his first four starts

## LARRY BROWN
*✴ Number 24 ✴*
Cornerback — 5-11 — 185

**BIRTHDATE:** 11-30-69 (Los Angeles, California)

**COLLEGE:** Texas Christian University

**MAJOR OR DEGREE:** Criminal Justice

**YEARS IN PROFESSIONAL FOOTBALL:** 2nd Season

**HONORS OR AWARDS:** All-City Selection in Both Football and Track at Los Angeles, California, High School; Named to the All-Southwest Conference and to the Blue/Gray All-Star Game, Earning Most Valuable Player Honors; Selected to the Pro Football Writers, Football News, Pro Football Weekly, and Football Digest All-Rookie Teams in 1991

**HOBBIES & INTERESTS:** Horseback Riding, Music, and Eating

## LARRY'S LEMON BUTTERMILK CAKE

| | |
|---|---|
| 1 c. shortening | 1/2 t. baking soda |
| 1 stick margarine | 1 T. hot water |
| 2-1/2 c. sugar | 4 eggs |
| 3-1/2 c. flour | |
| 1 t. lemon extract | 1/2 c. sugar |
| juice of 1 lemon | 1/2 c. *warm* water |
| 1 c. buttermilk | juice and rind of one |
| 1/2 t. salt | good-size lemon |

Cream shortening, margarine, and 2-1/2 c. sugar until all sugar grains disappear. Add eggs, one at a time; beat well after each addition. Add soda to hot water in spoon; mix. Add flour and liquids alternately to batter, beginning and ending with flour. Bake in an angel food tube cake pan (*be sure not to grease the pan*). Bake at 350 degrees for 1 hour and 15 minutes. Remove from pan immediately when done. Mix well 1/2 c. sugar and 1/c. *warm* water and the juice and rind of one good-size lemon. Pour over the hot cake. Cool completely before cutting, covering, or storing.

## BROWN'S THANKSGIVING BAKED SWEET POTATOES

| | |
|---|---|
| sweet potatoes, baking-size | 1/2 t. allspice |
| 1/2 c. butter | marshmallows |
| 1 c. brown sugar | pecans, whole |

Select baking-size sweet potatoes; wash, with or without skins. Trim ends off; wrap in foil. Bake at 350 degrees for 1 hour, or until soft. Remove from oven; cool until easily handled. Butter 9" x 13" baking dish. Slice sweet potatoes thickly; layer in bottom of baking dish. Melt butter over potatoes and sprinkle brown sugar over the casserole. Sprinkle allspice on top. On *each* slice, place a marshmallow and one whole pecan. Bake at 350 degrees until the marshmallows melt.

31

Larry earned Most Valuable Player honors in the Blue-Gray All-Star Game following his senior year at Texas Christian University

Larry -- one of the biggest surprises of training camp in 1991, earned a roster spot as a rookie on the strength of his athletic ability and speed

## LISA & TONY CASILLAS
### * *Number 75* *
### Defensive Tackle -- 6-3 -- 273

**BIRTHDATES:** *Tony* -- 10-26-63 (Tulsa, Oklahoma); *Lisa* -- 10-17-61 (Okmulgee, Oklahoma)

**COLLEGES:** *Tony* -- University of Oklahoma (B.A. -- Communications); *Lisa* -- University of Oklahoma (B.A. -- Psychology; Emory University School of Medicine (M.D.)

**GREATEST MOMENT IN SPORTS:** Shot 69 at St. Ives Country Club Golf Course

**GREATEST THRILL ABOUT BEING A PRO ATHLETE:** Being One of the Few of All the Kids Who Play Football to Make It to the Professional Level

**FAVORITE ACADEMIC SUBJECT:** *Tony* -- English, Drama; *Lisa* -- Biology

**WIFE'S OCCUPATION:** *Dr. Lisa Clayton* -- Medical Doctor, Specializing in Psychiatry

**HONORS OR AWARDS:** *Tony* -- 1984-1985 Consensus All-American; Won the Lombardi Trophy in 1985; All-Rookie Team in 1986; Second Team All-Pro in 1989

**HOBBIES & INTERESTS:** *Tony* -- Golf, Thoroughbred Horse Racing, and Acting; in 1991, Served as a Spokesman for the Austin Police Department in an Effort to Educate Youngsters as to the Dangers of Joining a Gang; *Lisa* -- Tennis (Plays in Local Leagues)

**FAVORITE AUTHOR:** *Tony* -- John Grisham; *Lisa* -- Any Mystery Writer

**FAVORITE TYPE OF MUSIC:** *Tony* -- Rock 'n Roll; *Lisa* -- Pop, Jazz, and New Country

**FAVORITE FOOD:** *Tony* -- All Mexican and Italian Food; *Lisa* -- Appetizers!

**FAVORITE TV/MOVIE STAR:** *Lisa* -- Angela Lansbury

**PET:** Dog -- Bo Bo

34

## TONY CASILLAS' STEW

1 lb. ground beef
2 T. margarine
1 small onion, chopped
1 t. chili powder
salt and pepper, to taste
1 c. macaroni
1 can tomatoes (15-oz.)
1 can ranch-style beans (15-oz.)

Brown ground beef, onion, and margarine. Add chili powder, salt and pepper; simmer. Cook macaroni separately in salted water. Drain macaroni. Combine meat mixture, tomatoes, beans, and cooked macaroni. Add water as necessary. Simmer for 20 minutes.

## LISA'S PICADILLO

2 lbs. ground beef
1/2 large onion, chopped
1 clove garlic, minced
1/2 green pepper, sliced
2 t. salt, scant
1/4 t. pepper
1 jalapeno, chopped
1 can whole tomatoes (28-oz.)
1/4 c. water
2 potatoes, cooked in microwave and chopped

Spray skillet with Pam Spray. Brown the ground meat with the onions. Add garlic and green pepper; stir over heat and brown. Add whole tomatoes, water, and jalapenos. Add potatoes; stir. Cover; simmer for 30 minutes.

The boy on the left is Tony (at 2 years of age)

Lisa and Tony Casillas, seeing their horses race at Remington Park, Oklahoma

Lisa, a medical doctor specializing in psychiatry, and Tony, one of
the Cowboy's most versatile performers

## SECOLA & DIXON VOLDEAN EDWARDS
## * *Number 58* *
## Linebacker — 6-1 — 224

**BIRTHDATES:** *Dixon* — 3-25-68 (Cincinnati, Ohio); *Secola* — 1-18-68 (Flint, Michigan)

**COLLEGES:** *Dixon* — Michigan State University (Building Construction Management); *Secola* — Michigan State University (Communication - Broadcast Journalism

**GREATEST MOMENT IN SPORTS:** Interception against Cincinnati Bengals for Touchdown

**GREATEST THRILL ABOUT BEING A PRO ATHLETE:** Just the Thrill of Being a Pro

**FAVORITE ACADEMIC SUBJECT:** *Secola* — Writing and Journalism Courses

**WIFE'S OCCUPATION:** Housewife

**HONORS OR AWARDS:** *Dixon* — Earned All-District and Team Most Valuable Player Honors, as a Tight End and Defensive Tackle in High School; First Season (1989), as Starting Weak-Side Linebacker, Earned Honorable Mention All-America Honors; Shared the Spartans Defensive Player of the Year Award, as a Senior; *Secola* — 1990 "Who's Who in America"; 1991 Governor's Award for Student Achievement

**HOBBIES & INTERESTS:** *Dixon* — Music, Rims and Tires, Fast Cars, and Home Improvement; *Secola* — Tennis, Fashion, Reading, and Politics

**FAVORITE AUTHOR:** *Dixon* — Anyone Who Contributes to "Low Rider" or "Architectural Digest"; *Secola* — Sidney Sheldon

**FAVORITE TYPE OF MUSIC:** *Dixon* — Rap; *Secola* — Ballads

**FAVORITE SPORTS HERO:** *Dixon* — "My Dad"; *Secola* — Husband Dixon (*Marcus Allen, a Close Second*)

**FAVORITE TV/MOVIE STAR:** *Secola* — Julia Roberts / Eddie Murphy (Tie)

**FAVORITE FOOD:** *Dixon* — Any Cake That's Extra Moist; *Secola* — Chinese (Bruno's Special)

**PET PEEVE:** *Dixon* — Hypocrites

**WORST FEAR:** *Dixon* — Fear of Failure

**CHILDREN & AGES:** Dixon Voldean, IV; and Taylor Sierra Lyn (Twins) - 14 mon.

## DIXON'S CINCY SANDWICHES

1-1/2 lb. boneless, skinless chicken breasts
1 bell pepper, chopped
1 onion, chopped
1 can mushrooms, drained and chopped (8-1/2 oz.)
1 T. Worcestershire sauce
1 T. margarine
1 T. seasoned salt
1/2 T. chicken (poultry) seasoning
2 T. pepper
1 t. garlic salt
1 pkg. favorite buns

Saute onions, peppers, mushrooms, and chicken (thinly-sliced); brown in skillet. Combine sauteed vegetables with Worcestershire sauce, seasoned salt, poultry seasoning, pepper, and garlic salt; mix completely. Combine vegetable mixture with chicken; let cook for 20-30 minutes on low heat. Adorn buns with favorite dressing. Fill buns with chicken. Enjoy! Makes 4-6 sandwiches. *Serving suggestion: Top with Cheddar cheese (melted).*

## SECOLA'S WINTER WONDERLAND CAKE

1 box of any *white* cake mix
3 egg whites
1/3 c. vegetable oil
2 large bananas, sliced
1 pkg. banana pudding
1 pkg. favorite gelatin, red in color
2 containers Cool Whip (12-oz. container)
1 c. strawberries or Maraschino cherries

Prepare cake mix as directed on box. Let cool completely. Take a fork; gently poke holes through entire cake. Prepare gelatin; pour over cake. Prepare pudding; spread over gelatin-soaked cake. Slice bananas; place over pudding. Spread Cool Whip over bananas (should be thick). Decorate cake with cherries or strawberries. Let sit at least 1 hour before serving.

## EDWARDS' GREEN BEAN CASSEROLE

2 cans green beans (French-style), drained
1 can cream of mushroom soup
1 bell pepper, sliced
1 large onion, sliced
seasoned salt, to taste
pepper, to taste

Preheat oven to 350 degrees. In small casserole dish, place 1 can of beans; top with 1/2 portion of peppers and onions. Top vegetables with 1/2 can mushroom soup. Repeat with remaining ingredients; top with pepper and seasoned salt. Bake for 20-30 minutes. Let stand 10 minutes before serving.

The fourth linebacker taken in the 1991 draft, Dixon was selected with the highest choice Dallas has used on a linebacker since 1984

Edward's twins: Dixon Voldean, IV; and Taylor Sierra Lynn - 14 months

Secola and Dixon -- who figures into the team's plans at outside linebacker for the future -- both attended Michigan State University

## ARIS & KENNETH GANT
### * *Number 29* *
### Cornerback -- 5-11 -- 191

**BIRTHDATES:** *Kenneth* -- 4-18-67 (Lakeland, Florida); *Aris* --(None Given)

**COLLEGES:** *Kenneth* -- Albany State College (Criminal Justice); *Aris* -- Albany State College

**YEARS IN PROFESSIONAL FOOTBALL:** 3rd Season

**HONORS OR AWARDS:** *Kenneth* -- Four-Year Starter for the Golden Rams of Albany State College; Earned All-Southern Intercollegiate Athletic Conference Honors for Three Years; Earned a Game Ball Award for His Special Teams Play vs. Cincinnati in 1991

**HOBBIES & INTERESTS:** *Kenneth* -- Playing Drums, Driving Go-Carts, and Eating; *Aris* -- Singing

## KENNETH'S ANGEL BISCUITS

| | |
|---|---|
| 5 c. flour | 1 c. shortening |
| 1/4 c. sugar | 1 yeast cake |
| 2 t. baking powder | 1 pkg. dry yeast |
| 1 t. baking soda | 2 T. warm water |
| 1 t. salt | 2 c. buttermilk |

1/2 c. margarine, melted (roll biscuits in this)

Sift dry ingredients together; blend in shortening. Dissolve yeast in warm water; let stand for 5 minutes. Add to buttermilk. Add this mixture to the flour mixture; blend well. Turn out on floured surface; roll to desired thickness. Cut biscuits; dip in melted margarine. Place on a greased pan. Bake at 450 degrees for 12 minutes. (*Note: The biscuits can be baked at once, or let rise a few minutes before baking. You can also go ahead and make the biscuits and cover with foil and freeze. Dough will keep in refrigerator for a few days, and you can make them up as needed.*)


## ARIS' SWISS CHEESE AND GREEN BEANS

2 cans French-style green beans
2 T. margarine, melted
2 T. flour
1 t. salt
2 t. sugar
4 t. onion, minced
1/2 pt. sour cream
Swiss cheese (8 oz.)
2 T. cornflakes, crushed

Cook and drain cans of French-style green beans. Mix together melted margarine, flour, salt, and sugar; add onion and sour cream. Mix green beans with sour cream mixture. Pour into casserole dish; cover with shredded Swiss cheese. Top with crushed cornflakes. Heat at 350 degrees until heated throughout (*do not let topping of cornflakes burn*).

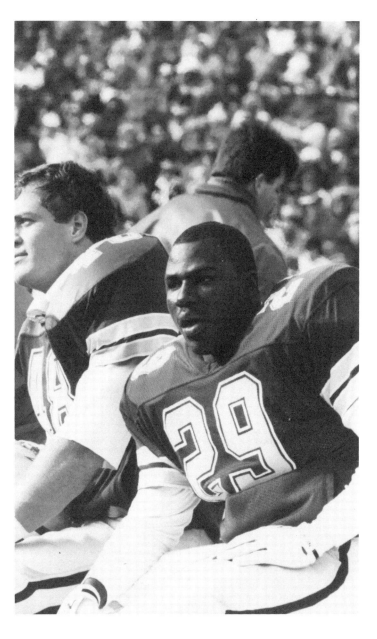

Last year, Gant established himself as one of the NFL's premier special teams players

Kenneth Gant -- the first player from Albany State to ever play for Dallas

# GINA & JOHN CHRISTIAN GESEK, JR.
## * *Number 63* *
### Guard -- 6-5 -- 279

**BIRTHDATES:** *John* -- 2-18-63 (San Francisco, California); *Gina* -- 1-14-65 (San Jose, California)

**COLLEGES:** *John* -- Cal State University (Sacramento); *Gina* -- Cal State University (B.A. -- Liberal Studies, Multiple Subject Credential)

**GREATEST THRILL ABOUT BEING A PRO ATHLETE:** Being Able to Use My Professional Athletic Platform to Help Others

**FAVORITE ACADEMIC SUBJECT:** *John* -- History and Political Science; *Gina* -- English, Art, and Classes Related to Teaching

**WIFE'S OCCUPATION:** Teacher by Trade; Homemaker by Choice

**HONORS OR AWARDS:** *John* -- All-Western Football Conference Lineman, as a Senior, at Cal State-Sacramento; Team Captain of the 1986 Western Football Conference Championship Team; Received Honorable Mention All-America Honors; *Gina* -- Honor Student

**HOBBIES & INTERESTS:** *John* -- Hunting, Fishing, and Golf; Enjoy Working on Home and Spending Time with Family; *Gina* -- Children's Advocate; Focus Volunteer Working with Children in the Court System Due to Abuse or Neglect

**FAVORITE AUTHOR:** *John* -- Tom Clancy and Neil Sperry; *Gina* -- Sidney Sheldon and Dr. James Dobson

**FAVORITE TYPE OF MUSIC:** *John* -- Easy Rock, Country, and Disney Sing-Alongs; *Gina* -- East Listening, Contemporary Christian, Country and Western, and Oldies

**FAVORITE SPORTS HERO:** *Gina* -- Husband John

**FAVORITE TV/MOVIE STAR:** *John* -- Gene Hackman and Tom Selleck; *Gina* -- Gene Hackman, Goldie Hawn, and Steve Martin

**FAVORITE FOOD:** *John* -- Prime Rib; *Gina* -- All Kinds!

**PET PEEVE:** *John* -- People Who Are Late . . . or Being Late; *Gina* -- People Who Don't Stand Up for What They Believe in

**WORST FEAR:** *John* -- "Anything Harming My Family"

**CHILDREN & AGES:** Tanner Christian -- 20 mon.

46

## JOHN'S SAN FRANCISCO BRUNO

1-1/2 lb. ground sirloin or chuck    6-8 eggs, beaten
10-15 cloves garlic, diced    salt and pepper
1 pkg. frozen chopped spinach (10-oz.)   1 can mushrooms, or fresh (4-oz.)

Brown ground beef. Add garlic. Add salt and pepper. Add spinach, stirring until spinach is soft. Add mushrooms. Bring to boil; turn to medium heat. Drain juice. Add eggs; mix thoroughly, allowing eggs to cook completely. Serve with salad and French bread.

## GINA'S BROWNIE TORTE

*Brownie:*    1 pkg. Pillsbury Fudge Browning Mix (21.5-oz.pkg.)
     1/2 c. water    1/2 c. oil    1 egg

Heat oven to 350 degrees. Grease bottom and sides of springform pan (9" or 10"). Combine all brownie ingredients in a large bowl; Beat 50 strokes by hand. Spread batter in greased pan. Bake at 350 degrees for 38-45 minutes, or until center is set. Cool for 30 minutes. Run knife around sides of pan to loosen; remove sides of pan. Cool completely.

*Filling:*    1 pkg. frozen raspberries in syrup, thawed (10-oz.)
     1 T. sugar
     1 T. cornstarch
     1 c. fresh raspberries, or frozen whole
       raspberries without syrup, thawed, drained
       on paper towel (*reserving 3 for garnish*)

Place thawed raspberries in syrup in blender container or food processor bowl with metal blade. Cover; process until pureed. Strain to remove seeds. In small saucepan, combine sugar and cornstarch. Gradually add raspberry puree. Mix well. Bring to a boil; cook until mixture is clear, stirring constantly. Cool for 5 minutes. Spread over brownie layer to within 1/2" of edges. Arrange 1 c. fresh raspberries evenly over raspberry mixture. Refrigerate.

*Topping:*    1 pkg. cream cheese, softened (8-oz.)
     1/3 c. powdered sugar
     2 T. white creme de cocoa, if desired
     1 c. vanilla milk chips, melted
     1 c. whipping cream, whipped

In medium bowl, combine cream cheese, powdered sugar and creme de cocoa; beat until smooth. Add melted vanilla chips; beat until smooth. Fold in whipped cream. Cover; refrigerate for 45 minutes.

*Garnish:*    1 T. semi-sweet chocolate, grated
     3 whole fresh, or frozen, raspberries, if desired
     3 mint leaves, if desired

Stir topping mixture until smooth. Spread 1-1/2 c. of the topping over raspberries. Spoon on remaining topping. Refrigerate at least 1 hour, or until firm. Sprinkle grated chocolate in 1" border around outside edge of torte. Garnish center with 3 whole raspberries and 3 mint leaves. Store in refrigerator. Makes 16 servings.

Gina, Tanner, and John on Tanner's new playground set.

Gina and Tanner, 20 months, at their home in Coppell, Texas

John Gesek majored in Physical Education at Cal State - Sacramento

John and Gina on a NFL Sports Cruise

## HEATHER & KEVIN PATRICK GOGAN
### * *Number 66* *
### Guard / Tackle -- 6-7 -- 319

BIRTHDATES: *Kevin* -- 11-2-64 (San Francisco, California); *Heather* -- 10-03-65 (San Francisco, California)

COLLEGES: *Kevin* -- University of Washington (Sociology); *Heather* -- University of Washington (Sociology)

GREATEST MOMENT IN SPORTS: Being Drafted by the Dallas Cowboys

GREATEST THRILL ABOUT BEING A PRO ATHLETE: Playing in a Big Game

FAVORITE ACADEMIC SUBJECT: *Kevin* -- Criminal Justice; *Heather* -- Sociology / Family Issues

WIFE'S OCCUPATION: Mother and Housewife

HONORS OR AWARDS: *Kevin* -- Led Sacred Heart High School in San Francisco to Two City Championships, as an Offensive and Defensive Tackle; Earned Honorable Mention All-PAC 10 Honors, as a Junior; Honorable Mention All-America and Second-Team All-PAC 10 Pick in Senior Year; Served as Team Co-Captain, as a Senior; Played in the 1987 Hula Bowl

HOBBIES & INTERESTS: *Kevin* -- Classic Cars and Fishing; *Heather* -- Outdoors, Hiking, Biking, and Flowers

FAVORITE AUTHOR: *Kevin* -- Ann Rule; *Heather* -- John Grisholm and Sue Grafton

FAVORITE TYPE OF MUSIC: *Kevin* -- Country; *Heather* -- Everything!

FAVORITE SPORTS HERO: *Kevin* -- Thurman Munson

FAVORITE TV/MOVIE STAR: *Kevin* -- Joe Pesci and Danny Glover

FAVORITE FOOD: *Kevin* -- Pizza; *Heather* -- Pizza and Pastries

CHILDREN & AGES: Hannah Belle - 8 mon.; Expecting Second Child in February

50

## KEVIN GOGAN'S SPECIAL OCCASION COOKIES

2-1/4 c. flour
1/4 t. salt
2 t. baking powder
1/2 c. shortening
1 c. sugar
2 eggs, beaten
1/2 t. vanilla
1 T. milk

Sift dry ingredients together. Separately cream shortening and sugar. Add eggs and vanilla; mix well. Mix with dry ingredients. Roll out on a lightly floured surface; cut into desired shapes. Bake at 375 degrees for 12 minutes. Decorate.

### HEATHER'S CHICKEN SALAD

1 head of lettuce, shredded
4 chicken breasts, shredded or cut into bite-size pieces
3-6 green onions, sliced into fairly-small pieces
almonds, sliced and toasted
sesame seeds, toasted
chow mein noodles, dry and crunchy

In a large bowl, put all salad ingredients, except chow mein noodles. Top with dressing; mix well. Serve chow mein noodles on the side; sprinkle on the top of individual servings.

*Dressing:*     4 T. sugar
                4 T. vinegar
                2 t. salt
                1/2 t. pepper
                1 c. oil

Combine all ingredients, except oil, in saucepan; dissolve over low heat. Remove from heat; add oil. Put on salad mixture.

Heather and Hannah, with family dogs

Kevin, who is generally considered to be one of the offensive line's most gifted natural athletes, holds daughter, Hannah - 18 months

Kevin Gogan has played every position on the Dallas' offensive front except center

## JAMISE & ALVIN CRAIG HARPER
*\* Number 80 \**
Wide Receiver -- 6-3 -- 207

**BIRTHDATES:** *Alvin* -- 7-7-67 (Frostproof, Florida); *Jamise* -- 10-7-68 (Murfreesboro, Tennessee)

**COLLEGES:** *Alvin* -- University of Tennessee (Psychology); *Jamise* -- University of Tennessee (B.S. -- Finance)

**GREATEST MOMENT IN SPORTS:** First NFL Touchdown -- Hail Mary Pass -- 1991 Season (Dallas vs. Redskins)

**GREATEST THILL ABOUT BEING A PRO ATHLETE:** Being a Role Model to Young Children

**FAVORITE ACADEMIC SUBJECT:** *Alvin* -- Sociology; *Jamise* -- Black American Literature

**WIFE'S OCCUPATION:** Accountant

**HONORS OR AWARDS:** *Alvin* -- Earned All-America Honors at Frostproof High School; Set the Florida State High Jump Record with a Leap of 7' 1"; at Tennessee, Won the High Jump Title in the 1989 SEC Indoor Meet with a Personal Best Jump of 7' 2-1/2"; Set the 1990 Indoor High Jump Record with 7' 3-1/2"; Two-Time All-Southeastern Conference Pick; Most Valuable Player at the Senior Bowl; Set a New School Record for Touchdown Receptions, as a Senior, at the University of Tennessee; Third on the All-Time Receiving List

**HOBBIES & INTERESTS:** *Alvin* -- Basketball, Reading, Television, and Golf

**FAVORITE AUTHOR:** *Alvin* -- Stephen King; *Jamise* -- Danielle Steel

**FAVORITE TYPE OF MUSIC:** *Alvin* -- Rap and Jazz; *Jamise* -- Rhythm and Blues

**FAVORITE SPORTS HERO:** *Alvin* -- Lynn Swann, Harold Carmichael, and Dr. J; *Jamise:* -- Husband Alvin

**FAVORITE TV/MOVIE STAR:** *Alvin* -- Eddie Murphy; *Jamise* -- Whoopi Goldberg

**FAVORITE FOOD:** *Alvin* -- Fried Chicken and Buffalo Wings; *Jamise* -- Pasta (Spaghetti)

**HOW THEY MET:** Met during Their Freshman Year at the University of Tennessee

## ALVIN'S HOMEMADE CHICKEN POT PIE

1 can of canned chicken
1 can of mixed vegetables
1 can of cream of chicken soup
2 frozen deep-dish pie shells, slightly-thawed
salt and pepper, to taste

Preheat oven to 350 degrees. Mix above ingredients. Add salt and pepper. Pour mixture in one of the pie shells. Place the remaining pie shell on top, removing the aluminum pan. Wet your hands with warm water; press firmly around the edges of the pie to seal. Cook pie for 45 minutes to 1 hour, or until top is a golden brown.

## JAMISE'S 7-UP APPLE DUMPLINGS

apples, diced (about 4 medium apples)
1 can biscuits, rolled thin (large can -- 10 biscuits)

Put apples in biscuits; twist tops to close.

*Boil:*
 1-1/2 c. 7-Up
 1 c. brown sugar
 1-1/2 t. cinnamon
 1/2 t. nutmeg
 1 stick margarine

Let boil; simmer for 5 minutes. Place dumplings in a glass baking dish. Pour mixture over the dumplings. Bake at 350 degrees for 45 minutes.

Alvin and Jamise Harper at the Tokyo trip "welcome party" in August, 1992

Shown in the summer of 1992, the Harpers met during their freshman year at the University of Tennessee

Alvin and Jamise's wedding day in Las Vegas, Nevada, on June 20, 1992

## BROOKE & DALE ROBERT HELLESTRAE
### * *Number 70* *
### Guard/Center -- 6-5 -- 283

**BIRTHDATES:** *Dale* -- 7-11-62 (Phoenix, Arizona); *Brooke* -- 11-28-63 (Phoenix, Arizona)

**COLLEGES:** *Dale* -- Southern Methodist University (Physical Education); *Brooke* -- Phoenix College

**GREATEST MOMENT IN SPORTS:** Starting and Playing in the AFC Championship Game with Buffalo

**GREATEST THRILL ABOUT BEING A PRO ATHLETE:** Working with Forty-Six Other Players toward a Common Goal -- *Winning!*

**FAVORITE ACADEMIC SUBJECT:** *Dale* -- Finance

**WIFE'S OCCUPATION:** Housewife and Mother; Owns "Cookies by Design" Shop in Scottsdale, Arizona

**HONORS OR AWARDS:** *Dale* -- All-State Pick in Football and Basketball at Saguaro High School in Scottsdale, Arizona; Earned All-Southwest Conference Honors, as a Senior, in 1984; Participated in the Cotton, Sun, and Aloha Bowls

**HOBBIES & INTERESTS:** *Dale* -- Golf, Basketball, and Racquetball; *Brooke* -- Avid Racquetball Player (*Very Competitive!*); Loves to Golf, Aerobics, Jog (Actually All Sports); Plays the Cello; Has Been a Singer since a Young Age; Crazy about Spending Time with Dale and Hillary (*"They're Great!"*)

**FAVORITE AUTHOR:** *Brooke* -- Anne Ortlund

**FAVORITE TYPE OF MUSIC:** *Dale* -- Country and Western; *Brooke* -- All Types (*Even a "Little" Country!*)

**FAVORITE SPORTS HERO:** *Dale* -- Walt Frazier; *Brooke* -- Husband Dale

**FAVORITE TV/MOVIE STAR:** *Dale* -- Clint Eastwood; *Brooke* -- Steve Martin and Goldie Hawn

**FAVORITE FOOD:** *Dale* -- Mexican; *Brooke* -- Ice Cream

**CHILDREN & AGES:** Hillary Royce -- Born 2-17-92

58

## DALE'S FLOUR CHICKEN ENCHILADAS

1 medium onion, diced
3 c. cooked chicken, chopped
1 T. butter or margarine, melted
1 jar sliced mushrooms, drained (4-oz.)
1 container sour cream (8-oz.)
1 can cream of chicken soup, undiluted
1 can green chilis, chopped and drained (4-oz.)
1/2 t. dried, whole oregano
1/4 t. salt
1/4 t. pepper
10 flour tortillas (7")
1 c. sharp Cheddar cheese, shredded (4 oz.)
1/3 c. milk

Saute onion in butter in a large saucepan until tender. Stir in the next nine ingredients, mixing well. Spoon about 1/2 c. chicken mixture in the middle of each tortilla. Roll up tortilla; place, seam side down, in a lightly-greased glass baking dish (9" x 13" x 2"). Combine remaining ingredients; spoon over tortillas. Sprinkle some cheese on top. Bake (uncovered) at 350 degrees for 35 minutes. Serves 5 people.

## BROOKE'S FROZEN CHERRY SALAD

1 pkg. cream cheese, softened (8-oz.)
1 c. sour cream
1/4 c. sugar
1/4 t. salt
2 c. miniature marshmallows
3/4 c. pecans
1 can crushed pineapple (8-3/4 oz.)
Mandarin orange slices (4 oz.)
1 can dark, sweet, pitted cherries (16-oz.)
whipping cream

Beat together cream cheese, sour cream, sugar, and salt. Drain all fruit; fold in with the first mixture. Add the marshmallows and pecans. Pour into 9" x 9" x 2" dish and put in freezer overnight. Slice; serve on bed of lettuce. Top with whipped cream.

Brooke, who owns a "Cookie by Design" Shop in Scotsdale, Arizona, with daughter, Hillary - born February 17, 1992

Dale, who has provided Dallas with an experienced deep snapper, holding Hillary

The Hellestrae Family -- Hillary, Dale, and Brooke

## ANTONIO (TONY) LA VOSIA HILL
### * *Number 90* *
### Defensive End — 6-6 — 255

**BIRTHDATE:** 10-23-68 (Warren County, Georgia)

**COLLEGE:** Tennessee-Chattanooga (B.A. — Criminal Justice)

**GREATEST MOMENT IN SPORTS:** Beating Chicago in His First Playoff Game

**FAVORITE ACADEMIC SUBJECT:** History

**HONORS OR AWARDS:** Starred at Warren County High School in Camak, Georgia; Played in the Florida-Georgia and the North-South All-Star Games; Second-Team Pick in Basketball — Recruited by Tennessee-Chattanooga for Hoops; as a Senior, Captured the State Shot Put Title and Finished Fourth in the High Jump; Placed Third in the Discus in Junior Year; Second-Team All-Southern Conference Pick, in 1989 — Started Every Game and Led the Team in Sacks; Received Kodak All-America Honors

**HOBBIES & INTERESTS:** Swimming, Watching Television, and Pool

**FAVORITE AUTHOR:** Alex Haley

**FAVORITE TYPE OF MUSIC:** Rhythm and Blues

**FAVORITE SPORTS HERO:** Herschel Walker

**FAVORITE TV/MOVIE STAR:** Wesley Snipes

**FAVORITE FOOD:** Chicken

62

## TONY'S FRIED CHICKEN AND OX TAILS

chicken
ox tails
tenderizer
Accent
salt and pepper
flour
Mazola Corn Oil
onions
vinegar

Combine tenderizer, Accent, and salt and pepper; marinate chicken and ox tails overnight. Cover chicken with flour; brown in corn oil. Boil onions in water with ox tails for 1-1/2 hours. Pour in vinegar; simmer for 1 hour. Serve with rice and beans.

## EVONNE HILL'S ROAST BEEF

beef roast
Accent
salt and pepper

Season meat with Accent and salt and pepper. Cook in roasting pan for 1-1/2 hours at 450 degrees. Slice; pour gravy (drippings) over sliced meat. Cook for additional 45 minutes.

Tony Hill is only the second player from Tennessee-Chattanooga to make the Dallas Cowboys' roster

Tony has size, speed, and the type of quickness that may make him a very active pass rusher in the Cowboys' 4-3 scheme

## BURNEDEAN & ISSIAC HOLT, III
### * Number 30 *
### Cornerback -- 6-2 -- 201

**BIRTHDATES:** *Issiac* -- 10-4-62 (Birmingham, Alabama); *Burnedean* -- 3-10-64 (Greenville, Mississippi)

**COLLEGES:** *Issiac* -- Alcorn State University; *Burnedean* -- Alcorn State University (B.S. -- Health Science)

**FAVORITE ACADEMIC SUBJECT:** *Burnedean* -- Biology

**WIFE'S OCCUPATION:** Self-Employed

**HONORS OR AWARDS:** *Issiac* -- Birmingham Area Defensive Back of the Year, as a Senior, in High School; Set the NCAA Division I-AA Career Record with 24 Interceptions in Four Years as a Starter at Alcorn State; Named to the Kodak All-America Football Team and the All-Southwestern Athletic Conference Team; NFC Defensive Player of the Week; Dallas Cowboys 1990 Defensive Player of the Year; *Burnedean* -- National Dean's List, Miss Greenville High School (1981), and National Honor Society

**HOBBIES & INTERESTS:** *Issiac* -- Football and Most Sports; *Burnedean* -- Reading, Attempts at Writing Poetry and Short Essays, and Being in Charge of Self

**FAVORITE AUTHOR:** *Issiac* -- Bill Cosby; *Burnedean* -- Toni Morrison

**FAVORITE TYPE OF MUSIC:** *Issiac* -- Reggae; Rhythm, and Blues; *Burnedean* -- Depends on Mood (*Listen to Everything*)

**FAVORITE SPORTS HERO:** *Issiac* -- O. J. Simpson; *Burnedean* -- Jim Brown (*after Reading His Book*)

**FAVORITE TV/MOVIE STAR:** *Burnedean* -- Cicely Tyson and Regina Taylor

**FAVORITE FOOD:** *Issiac* -- Fried Pork Chops; *Burnedean* -- Cheesecake

**CHILDREN & AGES:** Brianna - 4 yrs.

66

## MARY'S LUSCIOUS ORANGE CAKE
### *(Mary is Issiac's Mother)*

3/4 c. Miracle Whip Salad Dressing  3/4 c. orange juice
1 two-layer yellow cake mix          3 eggs
1 envelope Dream Whip Whipped Topping Mix

Preheat oven to 350 degrees. Mix together all ingredients at medium speed with electric mixer for 2 minutes. Pour into greased and floured 10" fluted tube pan. Bake for 35-40 minutes, or until wooden pick inserted near center comes out clean. Let stand for 10 minutes; remove from pan. Cool. Serve with Orange Mallow Cream.

*Orange Mallow Cream:*

1 container Philadelphia Brand Soft Cream Cheese (8-oz.)
1 jar Kraft Marshamallow Creme (7-oz.)
1/2 c. sour cream                    2 T. orange juice

Mix cream cheese and marshmallow creme at medium speed with electric mixer until well-blended. Blend in sour cream and juice; chill. Serve with Luscious Orange Cake.

## CLENDEAN'S PEACH COBBLER
### *(Clendean is Burnedean's Mother)*

*Filling:*

1/4 lb. (1 stick) margarine or butter  1-1/2 c. sugar
8 ripe peaches, peeled, thinly-sliced  2 T. flour
1/2 c. water or brandy                 pinch of salt

*Crust:*

4 T. (1 stick) margarine or butter     1 t. baking powder
1/2 c. sugar                           1/2 t. salt
1 c. flour                             1/2 c. milk or juice

Preheat oven to 350 degrees. To prepare the filling, melt the margarine in a medium-sized saucepan over medium heat. Stir in the sugar, flour, and salt; mix well. Then add the peaches and water. Stir; heat thoroughly about 5 minutes. Pour into a greased deep casserole dish (9" x 9"); set aside. To prepare the crust, in a medium-sized mixing bowl, cream the margarine with the sugar. Add the flour, baking powder, salt, and milk; mix well. Pour the batter over the peaches; bake for about 1 hour, or until golden brown. Serve with vanilla ice cream. Makes 6-9 servings.

67

Burnedean, who is self-employed, at home in Dallas

Brianna Holt at 4-year-old birthday party

Issiac, the Cowboys' leading pass interceptor in each of the past two seasons, had four thefts last year to bring his career total to 21

## LESLIE & RAYMOND (RAY) ANTHONY HORTON
### * *Number 20* *
### Safety -- 5-11 -- 190

BIRTHDATES: *Ray* -- 4-12-60 (Tacoma, Washington); *Leslie* -- 11-16-60 (Olympia, Washington)

COLLEGES: *Ray* -- University of Washington (B.A. -- Sociology); *Leslie* -- University of Washington (B.A. -- Business)

GREATEST MOMENT IN SPORTS: Super Bowl XXIII (Cincinnati vs. 49'ers)

GREATEST THRILL ABOUT BEING A PRO ATHLETE Fulfilling a Childhood Dream

FAVORITE ACADEMIC SUBJECT: *Ray* -- History; *Leslie* -- Business; Government and Society

WIFE'S OCCUPATION: Domestic Engineer

HONORS OR AWARDS: *Ray* -- Earned All-America and All-PAC Honors at Washington; Played in the Hula and Senior Bowls in 1982

HOBBIES & INTERESTS: *Ray* -- Golf; *Leslie* -- Arts and Crafts, Aerobics, Weight Lifting, Golf, and Travel

FAVORITE AUTHOR: *Ray* -- Clive Cussler; *Leslie* -- Frank Perreth

FAVORITE TYPE OF MUSIC: *Ray* -- Talk Radio; *Leslie* -- Contemporary Christian

FAVORITE SPORTS HERO: *Ray* -- Fred Couples; *Leslie* -- Husband Ray

FAVORITE TV/MOVIE STAR: *Ray* -- Eddie Murphy; *Leslie* -- Bette Midler

FAVORITE FOOD: *Ray* -- Chinese; *Leslie* -- Chocolate Decadence

PET PEEVE: *Ray* -- Bad Drivers and Slow Golfers

WORST FEAR: *Ray* -- Hitting a Bad Shot on the 1st Tee

CHILDREN & AGES: Taylor -- 4 yrs.; Jarren -- 10 mon.

## RAY'S NORTHWEST BAKED SALMON

1 salmon, fresh or frozen (5-12 lbs.)
1 fresh lemon, thinly-sliced
1 onion, thinly-sliced
4-6 slices of bacon
salt and pepper

Rinse salmon in cool water. Sprinkle salt and pepper in cavity. Layer sliced lemons, onions, and bacon in cavity. Using butcher's string, tie around salmon to hold cavity closed. Pour table salt over the entire outside of the fish. Bake (uncovered) on rack in baking pan at 350 degrees for 1 to 1-1/2 hours, depending on the size of the fish.


## LESLIE'S APPLE-TO-ROUND PIZZA

*Crust:*   2 c. flour
1 t. salt
2/3 c. shortening
1/4 c. cold water

Sift flour and salt into mixing bowl. Cut shortening into flour until mixture is the consistency of coarse meal. Add water; mix until dough forms a ball. Roll dough between 2 sheets of wax paper. Fit crust into large round pizza pan.

*Filling:*   6-8 medium apples, peeled, cored, and sliced
2 T. lemon juice
1 T. flour
1/2 t. salt
3 T. lemon juice
1 t. cinnamon
1/2 t. nutmeg
1/2 c. sugar
4 T. butter

Fill pastry-lined pizza pan with apples. Sprinkle apples with lemon juice. Combine next 6 ingredients; sprinkle over apples. Dot with butter.

*Topping:*   1 T. flour
1/2 t. cinnamon
2 T. sugar
3 T. butter, softened

Combine all ingredients; spread over entire pizza. Bake at 325 degrees for 30-45 minutes, or until apples are tender. If top begins to brown too quickly, cover with aluminum foil.

71

Horton children: Taylor - 4 years; and Jarren - 10 months

Ray Horton, who has started all 46 of the games he's played in with Dallas since joining the club in 1989, with son, Jarren

Leslie, who met Ray in the college cafeteria line as freshmen at the University of Washington, with daughter, Taylor

## SANDY & MICHAEL JEROME IRVIN
### * Number 88 *
### Wide Receiver -- 6-2 -- 199

**BIRTHDATES:** *Michael* -- 3-5-66 (Ft. Lauderdale, Florida); *Sandy* -- 1-2-66 (Miami, Florida)

**COLLEGES:** *Michael* -- University of Miami (Major: Business Management; Minor: Communications)

**GREATEST MOMENT IN SPORTS:** Many . . . Can't Pick One ("I've Been Blessed")

**GREATEST THRILL ABOUT BEING A PRO ATHLETE:** Being around So Many Guys Truly Working for a Common Goal

**FAVORITE ACADEMIC SUBJECT:** *Michael* -- Math ("So I Can Add up My Money")

**WIFE'S OCCUPATION:** Housewife

**HONORS OR AWARDS:** *Michael* -- Earned All-State Honors at St. Thomas Aquinas High School; Fine Basketball Player -- Won Several Slam-Dunk Contests in the Florida Area While in College; Holds Miami Career Records for Catches, Receiving Yards, and Touchdown Receptions; 11 Touchdown Catches in 1986 -- Hurricanes' Record; Involved in Two of the Cowboys' Three Longest Plays in 1990 Giving Him Four of Dallas' Eight Longest Plays Since 1988; Other than Quarterbacks, No Other Cowboys Player Has Been Involved in More Than One of Those Big Plays; in 1988, Became the First Cowboys Rookie Wide Receiver to Start a Season-Opener Since Bob Hayes in 1965; in 1990, Led Dallas in Yards Per Catch and Had the Team's Longest Reception; in 1991, a Career-Best Season with Single Season Club Record Numbers for Receptions and Receiving Yards, Led NFC in Catches, and Led the NFL in Yardage; Eclipsed Bob Hayes' Club Record for 100-Yard Receiving Games with Seven in 1991; Earned Consensus All-Pro Recognition; Named the MVP of the Pro Bowl in First Appearance in Hawaii; His Finest Game of the Year -- 10-Catch, 169-Yard Outing vs. Atlanta with a 58-Yard TD Reception

**HOBBIES & INTERESTS:** Michael -- Playing Video Games; Sandy -- Spending Time with Michael, Movies, Going Dancing and Dinner

**FAVORITE AUTHOR:** *Michael* -- Mike Fisher (Sports Page)

**FAVORITE TYPE OF MUSIC:** *Michael* -- Hip Hop (Educated Rap); *Sandy* -- Luther Vandross

**FAVORITE SPORTS HERO:** *Sandy* -- Husband Michael

**FAVORITE TV/MOVIE STAR:** *Michael* -- Chuck Norris

**FAVORITE FOOD:** *Michael and Sandy* -- Seafood

**CHILDREN & AGES:** Myesha Beyonca - 2-1/2 yrs.

74

## MICHAEL'S SPICY OVEN-FRIED CATFISH

4 dressed, farm-raised catfish (about 7 oz. each)
1/4 c. yellow cornmeal
1/4 c. dry bread crumbs
1/2 t. salt, optional
1/2 t. paprika
1/2 t. garlic powder
1/8 t. cayenne pepper
1/8 t. ground thyme
1/2 c. skim milk
1/4 c. margarine, melted

Move oven rack to position slightly above middle of oven. Preheat oven to 450 degrees. Combine cornmeal, bread crumbs, salt, paprika, garlic powder, cayenne pepper, and thyme. Dip fish into milk; coat with cornmeal mixture. Place in 9" x 13" x 2" rectangular pan coated with vegetable cooking spray. Pour margarine over fish. Bake (uncovered) until fish flakes very easily with a fork (about 15-20 min.). Makes 4 servings.

*Tartar Sauce:* 1/2 c. light mayonnaise or salad dressing
     2 T. dill pickles, chopped
     1 T. onion, finely-chopped
     1 T. parsley, chopped
     2-3 T. lemon juice
     dash of hot pepper sauce

Combine all ingredients in small bowl; chill. Serve with fish. Makes about 1/2 c. sauce.

## SANDY'S LIGHT SHRIMP CREOLE

1 T. vegetable oil
3 T. margarine
1/2 c. green pepper, chopped
1/2 c. onion, coarsely-chopped
1/3 c. green onions, sliced
1 t. basil leaves
1/2 t. thyme leaves
1/2 t. garlic salt
1-1/2 lbs. shrimp, shelled and deveined
1 c. tomatoes, chopped
2 T. Teriyaki sauce
hot cooked rice

Heat oil and butter in 10" skillet over medium heat. Cook green pepper, onion, and green onion with basil, thyme, and garlic salt *until just tender*. Add shrimp; cook until shrimp turn pink (about 3 min.). Stir in tomatoes and Teriyaki sauce; cook for few minutes to blend flavors. Serve over rice. Makes 6 servings.

Sandy and Michael, who enjoyed a career-best season in 1991 with single season club record numbers for receptions and receiving yards

Myesha Beyonca Irvin -- 2-1/2 years old

Just a repeat of 1991 will make Irvin the first player in NFL history with consecutive seasons of 1,500-or-more yards

## TAMMY & JAMES WILSON (JIM) JEFFCOAT, JR.
### * *Number 77* *
### Defensive End -- 6-5 -- 274

**BIRTHDATES:** *Jim* -- 4-1-61 (Long Branch, New Jersey); *Tammy* -- 1-21-63 (Columbus, Ohio)

**COLLEGES:** *Jim* -- Arizona State University (B.S. -- Communications; M.B.A. -- Business Administration); *Tammy* -- Arizona State University

**GREATEST MOMENT IN SPORTS:** Winning First District Championship in Wrestling

**FAVORITE ACADEMIC SUBJECT:** *Jim* -- History; *Tammy* -- Anatomy

**YEARS IN PROFESSIONAL FOOTBALL:** 10th Season

**WIFE'S OCCUPATION:** Mom and Homemaker by Choice

**HONORS OR AWARDS:** *Jim* -- Received Key to Hometown City; High School Jersey (#79) Retired; New Jersey Sportswriters' Association Unsung Hero Award in 1991; Received All-PAC 10 Honors, College Defensive Lineman of the Year, and Honorable Mention All-America Honors in 1981-1982; Named to the All-Time Fiesta Bowl Team in 1991; Sports Illustrated NFC Player of the Week; ASU Hall of Fame; *Tammy* -- Miss Arizona Second Runner-Up

**HOBBIES & INTERESTS:** *Jim* -- Fishing, Reading, Writing, Bowling, Computer Buff, and Working with Special Olympics, Make-A-Wish Foundation, Leukemia Society, and Boys Clubs; *Tammy* -- Body-Building, Jogging, Child Development, and Crafts

**FAVORITE AUTHOR:** *Jim* -- Alex Haley; *Tammy* -- Cliff Sheets (*"Introduced Me to a New Way of Eating"*)

**FAVORITE TYPE OF MUSIC:** *Jim* -- Rhythm and Blues (Favorite Song -- Sam Cooke's "A Change Is Going to Come); *Tammy* -- Rhythm and Blues

**FAVORITE SPORTS HERO:** *Jim* -- Muhammad Ali; *Tammy* -- Magic Johnson

**FAVORITE TV/MOVIE STAR:** *Jim* -- Denzel Washington; *Tammy* -- Wesley Snipes

**FAVORITE FOOD:** *Jim* -- Chicken; *Tammy* -- Pasta

**CHILDREN & AGES:** Jaren James -- 5 yrs.; Jackson Dean and Jacqueline Nicole (Twins) -- 21 mon.

*Dallas Cowboys Wives' Cookbook*

## JIM'S REVISED SPICY NACHOS

1 pkg. tortilla chips, no-oil (baked, not fried -- *1 gram fat for 16 chips*) -- [*try Guiltless Gourmet Chips at Tom Thumb]*
2 c. Alpine Lace Cheddar Cheese (non-fat), grated --or Kraft Fat-Free Cheese slices (16 oz.)
1 lb. ground white skinless turkey
1 pkg. taco seasoning mix                    1/2 head of lettuce, chopped
salsa                                        1 large tomato, chopped


Cook ground turkey; set aside. Prepare taco mix, substituting turkey for ground beef. Spoon taco mixture over the chips. Sprinkle cheese on top. Heat in microwave for 3 minutes. Sprinkle lettuce and tomatoes on top. Top with hot salsa, if desired. Serves 6 (*fat: 1.53 grams; calories: 67*).


## TAMMY'S LOW-FAT ZITI AND TURKEY CASSEROLE

Ziti noodles, uncooked (8 oz.)          1/2 t. salt (optional)
1/4 c. liquid Butterbuds, plus 2 T.     1 T. liquid Butterbuds
1/4 c. Parmesan cheese                  1 t. garlic, minced (in a jar)
2 T. flour                              1 medium onion, chopped
1-1/4 c. skim milk                      1/4 t. ground pepper
2 egg beaters
1/2 lb. ground white meat skinless turkey, cooked and drained
1 large carrot, peeled and shredded (optional)
1 can stewed tomatoes, drained (14-1/2 oz. can)
2 c. Alpine Lace Non-Fat Mozzarella Cheese, grated (16 oz.) -- or Kraft Fat-Free Cheese Slices


Cook Ziti as package directs; drain and place in a large bowl. Add 1 t. liquid Butterbuds; toss until coated. Add 1 T. Parmesan; toss to coat and set aside. Spray 2-qt. casserole dish with non-fat cooking spray. Preheat oven to 350 degrees. In a medium saucepan, over low heat, combine the 1/4 c. liquid Butterbuds and flour. Whisk in milk until blended. Bring to a boil, stirring constantly; boil and stir for 1 minute. Remove from heat; let stand for 5 minutes. In a small bowl, blend egg beater with a little of the hot sauce. Stir in remaining 3 T. Parmesan cheese and 1/2 t. salt; set aside. In large pot, saute onion and garlic in 2 T. liquid Butterbuds (about 2-3 minutes). Add cooked and drained ground turkey. Add carrots and tomatoes; break up tomatoes with spoon. Bring to a boil over medium heat. Cook mixture, stirring occasionally (about 3 minutes). Remove pot from heat; stir in 1/4 t. salt and pepper. Cool for 5 minutes. Stir 1 c. grated cheese in rest of sauce. Mix in Ziti noodles. Pour the Ziti turkey sauce mixture into the prepared casserole dish. Sprinkle remaining grated cheese on top. Bake at 350 degrees for 30-45 minutes, or until cheese is melted and the casserole is heated through. Serves 8 (*fat: 2.36 grams per serving; calories: 253*).

Jim Jeffcoat -- who has played in more and started more NFL games
than any current Cowboys' player -- and wife, Tammy

The Jeffcoats have three children: Jaren - 5 years; and (twins) Jackson and Jacqueline - 21 months

# DARYL PETER JOHNSTON
## * *Number 48* *
### Fullback — 6-2 — 238

BIRTHDATE: 2-10-66 (Youngstown, New York)

COLLEGE: Syracuse University (B.A. — Economics)

FAVORITE ACADEMIC SUBJECT: Finance, Money, and Banking

GREATEST MOMENT IN SPORTS: First NFL Touchdown

GREATEST THRILL ABOUT BEING A PRO ATHLETE: Completion of Childhood Dream

YEARS IN PROFESSIONAL FOOTBALL: 4th Season

HONORS OR AWARDS: Named Western New York Player of the Year in 1983 While Playing for Lewiston-Porter High School in Youngstown, New York; Graduated First in Class of 290 Students with a 4.0 Grade-Point Average; All-America and All-East First-Team Pick in 1988; Received an Honorable Mention AP All-America; Co-Captain of the 1989 Syracuse Orangemen

HOBBIES & INTERESTS: Golfing, Skiing, and Jet Skiing

FAVORITE AUTHOR: Tom Clancy

FAVORITE TYPE OF MUSIC: New Wave

FAVORITE SPORTS HERO: Larry Csonka

FAVORITE TV/MOVIE STAR: Jack Nicholson and Clint Eastwood

FAVORITE FOOD: Italian

# JOHNSTON'S HERBED BUTTERFLIED LEG OF LAMB

1/2 c. dry red wine
1/2 c. olive oil
2 T. dry sherry
1 T. soy sauce
1 t. dried rosemary leaves
1 t. dried thyme leaves
2 garlic cloves, crushed
1 butterflied leg of lamb (5-6 lbs.)

In small bowl, combine wine, olive oil, sherry, soy sauce, rosemary, thyme, and garlic. Place lamb in large zipper-top bag. Add wine mixture; seal bag. Refrigerate 12-24 hours, turning occasionally. Preheat broiler. Drain meat; place in broiler pan, opening up flat. Broil 6" from heat source, for 30-35 minutes for medium rare, turning occasionally and basting with marinade. Remove from broiler; let stand for 5 minutes before carving. Serves 6-8 people.


## DARYL'S STRAWBERRY SHORTCAKE

2 c. flour
2 T. sugar
3 t. baking powder
1 t. salt
1/3 c. shortening
1 c. milk
butter

strawberries, sweetened and
sliced or mashed
whipping cream

Sift together flour, sugar, baking powder, and salt. Cut shortening in fine. Stir milk in just until blended. Spread dough in round cake pan (8"). Dot with butter. Bake until medium brown at 350 degrees for 12-15 minutes. Cut into wedges; cut in half. Cover one half with sweetened sliced or mashed strawberries. Add top; cover with more strawberries. Serve warm with whipped cream.

83

One of Daryl's favorite hobbies is skiing

Johnson is a key performer on special teams, leading all offensive players in special teams tackles with 10 last season

Daryl is a punishing runner and blocker who also does a lot of things as a receiver out of the backfield

## JIMMIE JONES
### * *Number 97* *
Defensive Tackle -- 6-4 -- 276

**BIRTHDATE:** 1-9-66 (Okeechobee, Florida)

**COLLEGE:** University of Miami (Business)

**YEARS IN PROFESSIONAL FOOTBALL:** 3rd Season

**GREATEST MOMENT IN SPORTS:** Winning the National Championship at the University of Miami in 1987

**GREATEST THRILL ABOUT BEING A PRO ATHLETE:** The Opportunity to Have a Positive Effect on Children as a Role Model

**FAVORITE ACADEMIC SUBJECT:** Business Law

**HONORS OR AWARDS:** Okeechobee High School Homecoming King in 1984; Named to the All-Rookie Teams as Selected by the U.P.I., The National, and the Pro Football Writers Association in 1990

**HOBBIES & INTERESTS:** Video Games and Drag Racing

**FAVORITE AUTHOR:** Tom Clancy

**FAVORITE TYPE OF MUSIC:** All the Bass I Can Stand -- the Louder the Better!

**FAVORITE SPORTS HERO:** Jerome Brown

**FAVORITE TV/MOVIE STAR:** Jasmine Guy

**FAVORITE FOOD:** Chicken

**PET PEEVE:** People Running Down Miami Hurricanes' Football Program

**WORST FEAR:** Being Moved to Offensive Line

**CHILDREN & AGES:** Jimmeria - 5 yrs.

## JIMMIE JONES' OKEECHOBEE FRIED CAT FISH

6 medium catfish, cleaned and dressed
1 t. salt
1 t. pepper
1 bottle hot sauce (2-oz.)
2 c. self-rising cornmeal
vegetable oil
lemon slices

Sprinkle catfish with salt and pepper; place in shallow dish. Add hot sauce. Marinate 1-2 hours in refrigerator. Place cornmeal in a plastic bag; drop in catfish (one at a time) and shake until completely coated with cornmeal. Fry in deep hot oil (375 degrees) until fish float to the top and are golden brown; drain well. Garnish with lemon slices. Makes 6 servings.

## JIMMIE'S FLORIDA SWAMP MUD CAKE

1 c. butter
1/3 c. cocoa
2 c. sugar
1-1/4 c. flour

4 eggs
1 t. vanilla
1 jar marshmallow creme (7-oz.)

Melt butter and cocoa together; cool. Blend sugar, flour, and eggs in a bowl. Add cooled cocoa mixture and vanilla. Bake in a 9" x 13" pan for 20-25 minutes at 375 degrees. After taking cake out of oven, spread marshmallow creme over the top. Wait 10 minutes; spread icing over the top. Sprinkle with nuts.

*Icing:* 1/2 lb. powdered sugar
1/2 cube butter
1/2 c. walnuts, chopped

4 T. cocoa
warm milk (a little)

Mix sugar, butter, and cocoa. Add warm milk until spreadable.

87

Jimmie with his pride and joy: a Mustang and a BMW

Daughter, Jimmeria, 5 years old, posing on Easter Sunday

Jimmie Jones (with hat on) with "The Temptations"

## LEON LETT
## * *Number 78* *
## Defensive Tackle -- 6-6 -- 292

BIRTHDATE: 10-12-68 (Fair Hope, Alabama)

COLLEGE: Emporia State University (Sociology)

GREATEST MOMENT IN SPORTS: Beating Chicago

GREATEST THRILL ABOUT BEING A PRO ATHLETE:
Draft Day

FAVORITE ACADEMIC SUBJECT: English

HONORS OR AWARDS: Starred in Football and Basketball
at Fair Hope, Mississippi, High School; Received an
Honorable Mention NAIA All-America, All-NAIA District 10,
and All-CSIC Honors in 1989; Twice Named District 10
Player of the Week as a Junior in College

FAVORITE AUTHOR: Alex Haley

FAVORITE TYPE OF MUSIC: Rhythm and Blues

FAVORITE SPORTS HERO: Ed "Too Tall" Jones

FAVORITE TV/MOVIE STAR: Wesley Snipes

FAVORITE FOOD: Italian, Especially Lasagna

## LEON'S SUNDAY CHICKEN AND RICE

1 pkg. onion soup mix
1 can cream of onion soup
1 small can mushroom pieces
1 c. uncooked yellow rice
1/2 can water (onion soup can)
8-10 pieces of chicken, cut into chunks

Butter 9" x 12" baking dish. Sprinkle onion soup mix on bottom of dish. Add rice and cut chicken. Pour in mushroom and water mixture. Cover tightly; bake at 350 degrees for 1-1/2 hours. Makes 4-6 servings.

## RACHAEL LETT'S CHOCOLATE MAYO CAKE

1 c. mayonnaise
2 t. baking soda
1 c. cold water
2 c. flour (not self-rising)
1 t. vanilla
1 c. sugar
1/2 c. cocoa
1/2 t. salt, optional

In bowl, mix together flour, sugar, cocoa, salt, and soda. In another bowl, mix together mayonnaise, water and vanilla. Combine mixtures in two bowls together until moist. Bake at 350 degrees for 30 minutes in 9" x 12" greased and floured baking dish. Serve frosted or plain.

Leon Lett is the first Emporia State player to ever play for Dallas

Blessed with tremendous size and athletic ability, Leon could blossom into a dominant force on the Dallas defensive line

## LYNN & KELVIN BRIAN MARTIN
### *Number 83*
Wide Receiver -- 5-9 -- 165

BIRTHDATES: *Kelvin* -- 5-14-65 (Jacksonville, Florida); *Lynn* -- 4-17-65 (Jacksonville, Florida)

COLLEGES: *Kelvin* -- Boston College (Communications); *Lynn* -- Florida State University (Merchandising)

GREATEST MOMENT IN SPORTS: Punt Return for a Touchdown against the Philadelphia Eagles in 1991 Season

WIFE'S OCCUPATION: Housewife

HONORS OR AWARDS: *Kelvin* -- Earned All-City and All-Conference Honors at Ribault High School in Jacksonville; Finished among the Nation's Top 10 Punt Returners in Each of His Final Three Seasons at Boston College; Led the Nation's Receivers in Yards Per Catch in 1985; Set Boston College Career Marks for Receptions, Receiving Yards, and Touchdown Catches; Leading Receiver for Cowboys in 1989 and 1990

HOBBIES & INTERESTS: *Kelvin* -- Bowling and Basketball; *Lynn* -- Reading, Bowling, and Exercising

FAVORITE TYPE OF MUSIC: *Kelvin and Lynn* -- Rhythm and Blues

FAVORITE SPORTS HERO: *Kelvin* -- Gayle Sayers; *Lynn* -- Husband Kelvin

FAVORITE TV/MOVIE STAR: *Kelvin* -- Wesley Snipes; *Lynn* -- Denzel Washington and Whoopi Goldberg

FAVORITE FOOD: *Kelvin* -- T-Bone Steak; *Lynn* -- Crab Cakes

CHILDREN & AGES: Kelvin Andrew -- 3 yrs.

94

## KELVIN'S PEACH COBBLER

2 c. peaches, sliced
3/4 c. flour
pinch of salt
2 T. baking powder
1 c. sugar
3/4 c. milk
1/2 c. butter or margarine
1/4 T. cinnamon

Sift flour, salt, and baking powder together. Mix with 1/2 c. sugar; slowly stir in milk to make batter. Put melted butter in baking pan (8" x 8" x 2"). Pour batter over butter (*do not stir*). Mix peach, cinnamon, and 1/2 c. sugar thoroughly; add to batter. Bake at 350 degrees for 1 hour.

## LYNN'S SHRIMP SALAD

1/2 lb. Creamettes medium shells, cooked and drained
1 pkg. frozen cooked shrimp, thawed and drained (10-oz.)
1-1/2 c. celery, chopped
3/4 c. mayonnaise, more or less -- depending upon taste
1/2 doz. eggs, hard-boiled and chopped
1 jar pimientos (2-oz.)
1/2 c. sweet pickles, chopped
seasoning salt
black pepper
red pepper, optional

Mix all ingredients together. Season with seasoning salt, black pepper, and red pepper (optional), to taste. Chill and enjoy.

Kelvin and Lynn Martin with Kelvin Andrew -- 3 years of age

Kelvin finished third in the NFL in punt returns last year with an 11.6 yard average, the highest finish by a Dallas Cowboy in 17 years

# RUSSELL MARYLAND
## * *Number 67* *
### Defensive Tackle — 6-1 — 275

**BIRTHDATE:** 3-22-69 (Chicago, Illinois)

**COLLEGE:** University of Miami (Psychology)

**GREATEST MOMENT IN SPORTS:** Beating University of Texas in 1991 Cotton Bowl in Senior Year

**GREATEST THRILL ABOUT BEING A PRO ATHLETE:** Positive Influence on Kids

**FAVORITE ACADEMIC SUBJECT:** Spanish

**HONORS OR AWARDS:** Starred as Two-Way Lineman in High School; Undefeated in "Big Man's 60-yard Dash," Which Was Open to Those Who Competed in the Field Events, in Which He Competed on the Track Team in the Shot Put; Played on Two-Time National Champions Miami Team in 1987 and 1989; Two-Time First-Team All-America at Miami; Winner of 1990 Outland Trophy; First Player Selected in 1991 NFL Draft; in 1991, Named NFL Rookie of the Year by Edelstein Pro Football Letter, Earned All-Rookie Honors from Pro Football Writers of America, Pro Football Weekly, and College & Pro Football Newsweekly

**HOBBIES & INTERESTS:** Listen to Music

**FAVORITE AUTHOR:** Langston Hughes

**FAVORITE TYPE OF MUSIC:** Rhythm and Blues

**FAVORITE SPORTS HERO:** Walter Payton

**FAVORITE TV/MOVIE STAR:** Eddie Murphy

**FAVORITE FOOD:** Chicken

**PET PEEVE:** Walking for Long Lengths of Time

**WORST FEAR:** Not Given the Chance to be the Best He Can Be

## RUSSELL'S CHICKEN BREAST SUPREME

4 whole chicken breasts, split
1/4 c. butter of margarine
2 c. mushrooms, sliced
2 cans of cream of chicken soup (10-1/2 oz. can)
1 large clove garlic, minced
dash of thyme
1/8 t. rosemary
2/3 c. light cream

Brown chicken breasts in butter; remove chicken. Brown mushrooms; stir in soup, garlic, and seasonings. Add chicken. Cover pot; cook on low heat for 45 minutes, or until tender. Blend in cream, while heating slowly. Serve with hot rice.

## RUSSELL'S AUNT DELORES' BARBECUE SHORT RIBS

3 lbs. beef short ribs, cut into serving pieces
2 T. shortening
1/2 c. onions, chopped
1 c. catsup
1/2 c. water
1/4 c. brown sugar, firmly-packed
3 T. Worcestershire sauce
2 t. prepared mustard
2 t. garlic salt
1/4 t. thyme
1 lemon slice

Brown meat in shortening in skillet; drain fat. Add remaining ingredients to skillet. Cover; simmer for 1-1/2 to 2 hours, or until tender (*or you can cover and bake at 350 degrees for 1-1/2 to 2 hours*).

99

Russell -- a consensus All-America and Outland Trophy winner at Miami in 1990

Russell Maryland -- selected as the No. 1 overall choice in the 1991 NFL Draft

## GODFREY MYLES
### * *Number 98* *
### Linebacker — 6-1 — 242

**BIRTHDATE:** 9-22-68 (Miami, Florida)

**COLLEGE:** University of Florida (Sociology)

**YEARS IN PROFESSIONAL FOOTBALL:** 2nd Season

**HONORS OR AWARDS:** Earned Second-Team All-State Honors at Carol City High School in Miami; Selected to Florida's 35-Man Super Squad That Met a Team of Georgia Prep All-Stars in the Summer of 1987; Named the "Most Underrated Player in the Country" by The Sporting News, Prior to His Junior Year; All-Southeastern Conference in 1990; Honorable Mention All-America Pick (1989-1990)

**HOBBIES & INTERESTS:** Lifting Weights and Listening to Music

## GODFREY'S LEMON PIE

1 prepared 9" one-crust pie shell
1 c. sugar
2 T. cornstarch
2 T. flour
1 c. water
2 egg yolks, beaten
1 T. margarine or butter
1/2 t. lemon peel, grated
1/4 c. lemon juice
1 c. vanilla milk chips, or white baking bar, chopped (6 oz.)
1 pkg. light cream cheese (Neufchatel), softened (8-oz.)
1/2 c. whipping cream, whipped
1 T. almonds, sliced and toasted

Preheat oven to 450 degrees. Prepare pie crust according to directions on the package. Bake until lightly-browned; cool thoroughly. In medium saucepan, combine sugar, cornstarch, and flour; mix well. Gradually stir in water until smooth; cook over medium heat until mixture boils, stirring constantly. Remove from heat. Stir about 1/4 c. of hot mixture into egg yolks; blend well. Add egg yolk mixture to mixture in saucepan; cook over low heat until mixture boils, stirring constantly. Cook for 2 minutes, stirring constantly. Remove from heat; stir in margarine, lemon peel, and lemon juice. Transfer 1/3 c. of hot filling to a small saucepan. Cool remaining lemon mixture for 15 minutes. Add vanilla milk chips (or white baking bar) to hot filling in small saucepan; stir over low heat, *just until chips are melted.* In small bowl, beat cream cheese until fluffy. Add melted vanilla milk chip mixture; beat until well-blended. Spread over bottom of cooled pie crust. Spoon lemon mixture over cream cheese layer. Refrigerate for 2-3 hours, or until set. In small bowl, beat whipping cream until stiff peaks form; spoon over pie. Garnish with toasted almonds. Store in refrigerator. Makes 8-10 servings.

Godfrey Myles -- the eighth linebacker selected in the 1991 draft

Myles named the "most underrated player in the country" by The Sporting News prior to his junior year at the University of Florida

# DOROTHY & NATHANIEL (NATE) NEWTON, JR.
## * Number 61 *
### Offensive Tackle — 6-3 — 303

**BIRTHDATES:** *Nate* — 12-20-61 (Orlando, Florida); *Dorothy* — 12-20-61 (New Orleans, Louisiana)

**COLLEGES:** *Nate* — Florida A & M University; *Dorothy* — University of Southwestern - Lafayette, Louisiana (Accounting and Sociology)

**GREATEST MOMENT IN SPORTS:** Watching the Birth of Nathaniel Newton, III; Playing Professional Football

**GREATEST THRILL ABOUT BEING A PRO ATHLETE:** Being Able to Compete Every Sunday

**FAVORITE ACADEMIC SUBJECT:** *Nate* — Reading; *Dorothy* — History

**WIFE'S OCCUPATION:** Loan Secretary at First Coppell Bank

**HONORS OR AWARDS:** *Nate* — Played on Both Offensive and Defensive Lines While Winning Four Letters at Florida A & M; as a Senior, Team Captain and Named All-Conference; Named Cowboys' Most Valuable Offensive Player by Pro Football Weekly; Only Dallas Offensive Lineman to Earn All-Pro Votes from Associated Press in 1990; Finished 1990 with a Team-High 39 Straight Starts; Named to All-Madden Team for the Second Straight Year; All-Negro League; All-Conference (MEAC); *Dorothy* — College on Academic and Volleyball Scholarship

**HOBBIES & INTERESTS:** *Nate* — Basketball, Collecting Video Movies, and Raising American Pit Bull Terriers; *Dorothy* — All Sports and Collecting Video Movies

**FAVORITE AUTHOR:** *Nate* — Louis L'Amour

**FAVORITE TYPE OF MUSIC:** *Nate* — All Music; *Dorothy* — Rhythm and Blues

**FAVORITE SPORTS HERO:** *Dorothy* — Husband Nate

**FAVORITE TV/MOVIE STAR:** *Dorothy* — Steven Seagal

**FAVORITE FOOD:** *Nate* — Potatoes (French Fries or Cooked in Several Different Ways); *Dorothy* — Mexican

**WORST FEAR:** *Nate* — Height and Large Bodies of Water

**CHILDREN & AGES:** Nathaniel, III (Tre) - 3 yrs.

## NATE'S CORN CASSEROLE

1 can whole kernel corn
1 can creamy corn
1 pt. sour cream
1 stick butter
1 box Jiffy Corn Bread Mix

Melt butter in casserole dish. Place butter in oven until it melts. Mix all remaining ingredients together. Pour ingredients in casserole dish with butter; mix together. Bake at 400 degrees until casserole is brown on top.

## DOROTHY'S CHEESECAKE

*Crust:*      1-1/2 c. graham cracker crumbs
              2 T. butter, melted
              2 T. sugar

*Cake:*       3 pkgs. cream cheese (8-oz. pkg.)
              1-1/2 c. sugar
              5 eggs
              1 t. vanilla

Combine graham cracker crumbs, melted butter, and sugar. Press on bottom of a springform pan. Beat cream cheese until smooth. Add sugar; beat until smooth. Add eggs and vanilla; beat until smooth. Pour into crust. Bake at 350 degrees for 1 hour. (*Amaretto can be substituted for vanilla.*)

Dorothy and Nate Newton met in Valley Ranch at Allstate Insurance and Sunbelt Savings -- both offices were in the same building

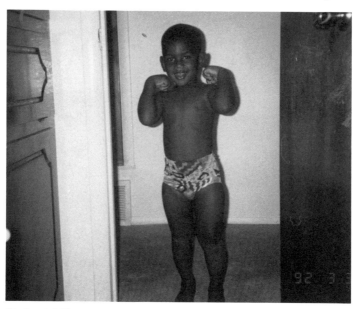

Nathaniel Newton, III -- Look at those muscles!

Nate, reading his favorite author, Louis L'Amour

"Look, I wear the same #61, Dad!"

# ANGELA & KEN NORTON, JR.
## * *Number 51* *
### Linebacker — 6-2 — 241

**BIRTHDATES:** *Ken* — 9-29-66 (Jacksonville, Illinois); *Angela* — 2-18-66 (Dallas, Texas)

**COLLEGES:** *Ken* — U.C.L.A. (Psychology); *Angela* — John Robert Powers Modeling School

**GREATEST MOMENT IN SPORTS:** Being Drafted in 1988; Playoffs in 1991 against Chicago; Beating the Redskins

**GREATEST THRILL ABOUT BEING A PRO ATHLETE:** Exciting Thrill Playing in a Big Game; Making Huge Play That Decides Outcome of Game

**FAVORITE ACADEMIC SUBJECT:** *Ken* — Psychology / History

**WIFE'S OCCUPATION:** Housewife and Mother

**HONORS OR AWARDS:** *Ken* — Only West Coast Nominee for Butkus Award in 1987; All-America Inside Linebacker at U.C.L.A.

**HOBBIES & INTERESTS:** *Ken* — Playing Pool, Reading, and Movies; *Angela* — Water Skiing and Traveling

**FAVORITE AUTHOR:** *Ken* — John Steinbeck

**FAVORITE TYPE OF MUSIC:** *Ken* — Rhythm and Blues; Jazz; *Angela* — Rhythm and Blues

**FAVORITE SPORTS HERO:** *Ken* — Dr. J; Willie Stargell; Dick Butkus; and Jesse Owens; *Angela* — Husband Ken

**FAVORITE TV/MOVIE STAR:** *Ken* — Bill Cosby and Denzel Washington; *Angela* — Ann Archer

**FAVORITE FOOD:** *Ken* — Chicken and Dumplings, Chicken and Dressing, Cranberry Sauce, Fried Chicken Drumsticks; *Angela* — Seafood

**CHILDREN & AGES:** Brittney - 6 yrs.

110

## KEN'S DELICIOUS CHOCOLATE SHEET CAKE

| | |
|---|---|
| 2 c. flour | 1/2 c. Wesson Oil |
| 2 c. sugar | 1/2 c. buttermilk |
| pinch salt | 1 t. baking soda |
| 4 T. cocoa | 2 eggs |
| 1 c. cold water | 1 t. vanilla |
| 1 stick butter or margarine | |

Sift flour, sugar, and salt together in a large bowl. Put cocoa, water, butter, and oil in saucepan; bring to boil. Pour over dry ingredients while hot. Dissolve baking soda in buttermilk. Add egg and vanilla; add to above mixture. Beat until smooth. Grease and flour large sheet pan. Pour mixture into pan. Bake for 18 minutes at 400 degrees.

*Icing:* 1 stick margarine        4 T. cocoa
      6 T. milk                    1 t. vanilla
      1 box powdered sugar (16-oz.)
      1 c. pecans

Beat ingredients together until smooth. Spread frosting over cooled cake.


## ANGELA'S GRANNY'S CHICKEN AND DUMPLINGS

| | |
|---|---|
| 1 whole chicken, cut-up | 4 large carrots, cut-up |
| 1 onion, chopped | salt and pepper |
| 4 stalks celery, cut-up | 1 doz. flour tortillas |

Cut up whole chicken; put in a large pot and cover with water. Add onion, celery, and carrots. Cook until chicken is done. Remove chicken and let cool; remove bones. Put chicken back into liquid with vegetables. Add salt and pepper. Bring to boil. *Here's the "secret" ingredient:* Cut up flour tortillas in large pieces; add to chicken and vegetables. Cook and stir until liquid thickens (about 5-10 minutes). *Enjoy!*

Ken Norton -- who started all 16 games last year and enjoyed a very productive season -- and his wife, Angela, met on a blind date

The Norton's daughter, Brittney - 6 years old

## YVETTE & JAY MCKINLEY NOVACEK
### * *Number 84* *
### Tight End — 6-4 — 231

**BIRTHDATES:** *Jay* — 10-24-62 (Martin, South Dakota); *Yvette* — 5-5-63 (Cozad, Nebraska)

**COLLEGES:** *Jay* — University of Wyoming (Major — Industrial Arts / Education); *Yvette* — University of Nebraska / Lincoln (B.S. — Agricultural Economics)

**GREATEST MOMENT IN SPORTS:** Competed in 1984 Olympic Trials — Decathlon

**FAVORITE ACADEMIC SUBJECT:** *Yvette* — Wildlife Management

**YEARS IN PROFESSIONAL FOOTBALL:** 8th Season

**WIFE'S OCCUPATION:** Financial Consultant

**HONORS OR AWARDS:** *Jay* — All-State Quarterback at Gothenburg High School in Nebraska (Coached by His Father); University of Wyoming Record Holder in Decathlon and Pole Vault; Won Western Atlantic Conference Championship in the Decathlon in 1984; Competed in Decathlon at 1984 U.S. Olympic Trials; All-American at University of Wyoming; Earned Second-Team All-NFC Recognition by UPI, While Being Named First-Team NFL All-Pro by "The Football News" and "College and Pro Football Weekly"; Last April Won Team Event and Had Highest Individual Score in NFL-National Cutting Horse Association Super Stakes; *Yvette* — Graduated *Magna Cum Laude*

**HOBBIES & INTERESTS:** *Jay* — Hunting, Fishing, Cutting Horses, and Dogs; Hosts One-Week Youth Football Camp during the Off-Season; Donates Time to Help the Party Smart Campaign and the Drug Abuse Resistance Education Program; *Yvette* — Cutting Horses; Baking Desserts

**FAVORITE AUTHOR:** *Jay* — Louis L'Amour

**FAVORITE TYPE OF MUSIC:** Country

**FAVORITE SPORTS HERO:** *Jay* — Mike Beers (Team Roper)

**FAVORITE FOOD:** *Yvette* — Desserts

**HOW THEY MET:** Met at a Street Dance in Yvette's Home Town (Eustis, Nebraska)

**PETS:** Horses — Sackett, Lady Blue, and Cola Doc; Dogs — Marlow and Teal; and Cats — Chaps and Spurs

## JAY'S SOUR CREAM POUND CAKE

2 sticks butter
3 c. sugar
6 eggs, separated
1 c. sour cream
3 c. flour
1/4 t. baking soda
1/2 t. salt
2 t. vanilla
2 t. almond extract

Cream butter and sugar thoroughly. Separate eggs. Beat egg whites until very stiff. Add egg yolks and sour cream to butter mixture. Add flavoring and dry ingredients. Gradually fold in beaten egg whites. Bake in two loaf pans at 300 degrees for 1 hour and 20 minutes.

*Variations:*

| | |
|---|---|
| *Chocolate* -- | add 2 oz. bitter chocolate and 1/3 c. chocolate syrup |
| *Mocha* -- | add 1/3 c. strong coffee and 3 T. Swiss Mocha instant coffee |
| *Coconut* -- | add 2 T. coconut flavoring and 1 c. coconut |
| *Lemon* -- | add 2 c. lemon extract and 1/3 c. lemon juice |

## YVETTE'S MILKY WAY CAKE

8 Milky Way candy bars
1 c. margarine
2 c. sugar
1-1/4 c. buttermilk
1/2 t. baking soda
4 eggs
2-1/2 c. flour
2 t. vanilla

Melt candy bars and margarine over low heat; let cool. Mix sugar, buttermilk, baking soda, eggs, flour, and vanilla; beat for 2 minutes. Fold in candy mixture. Bake at 350 degrees for 35-40 minutes, or until done.

*Frosting:*    cream cheese (8 oz.)
1 stick margarine
1 box powdered sugar

Cream ingredients together. Frost cake.

115

Jay and Yvette, with Jay's horse -- Sackett, after the NFL-NCHA cutting

Jay won the first annual NFL-NCHA cutting horse competition with a score of 219

The Novaceks dated long distance for five years -- here they are celebrating their 4th wedding anniversary

## ANGEL & ALFREDO ROBERTS
### * Number 87 *
Tight End -- 6-3 -- 252

**BIRTHDATES:** *Alfredo* -- 3-17-65 (Hollywood, Florida); *Angel* -- 11-17-64 (Chicago, Illinois)

**COLLEGES:** *Alfredo* -- University of Miami (B.A. -- Criminal Justice); *Angel* -- California State University Northridge (B.A. -- Communications)

**GREATEST MOMENT IN SPORTS:** First NFL Touchdown! Being Drafted by the Kansas City Chiefs

**FAVORITE ACADEMIC SUBJECT:** *Alfredo* -- Math; *Angel* -- Speech and Television Production

**WIFE'S OCCUPATION:** Advertising Media Coordinator

**HONORS OR AWARDS:** *Alfredo* -- All-City and Second-Team All-State Selection at South Plantation High School in Ft. Lauderdale, Florida; Second-Team All-State Catcher/First Baseman on the Baseball Team; Red-Shirt Freshman on 1983 Miami National Championship Squad; Rookie in 1988 -- Started First Seven Games of the Season; Became Kansas City Chiefs' Lowest-Round Draft Choice to Start on Opening Day since 1967

**HOBBIES & INTERESTS:** *Alfredo* -- Fishing and Bowling; *Angel* -- Running, Weights, and Spending Time with Husband

**FAVORITE AUTHOR:** *Alfredo* -- Alice Walker

**FAVORITE TYPE OF MUSIC:** *Alfredo* -- Rhythm and Blues; Soul; *Angel* -- Jazz

**FAVORITE SPORTS HERO:** *Alfredo* -- Ozzie Newsom and Paul Warfield; *Angel* -- Husband Alfredo

**FAVORITE TV/MOVIE STAR:** *Alfredo* -- James Earl Jones and Robert DeNiro; *Angel* -- Bill Cosby

**FAVORITE FOOD:** *Alfredo* -- Snap Green Beans, Fried Catfish with Grits; *Angel* -- Copeland's Cheesecake

**PET PEEVE:** *Alfredo* -- "I Always Have to Be Right!"

**WORST FEAR:** *Alfredo* -- "Competing against My Wife and Her Winning"

## AB'S BAKED BEANS DELIGHT

3 large cans of baked beans    1 whole white onion, cut-up
2 c. brown sugar, level        1 whole bell pepper, cut-up
1/2 c. yellow mustard          3 strips bacon
1 c. catsup

In a large bowl, combine all of the above ingredients, except bacon. Stir until all ingredients are well-mixed. Use a large cake pan; pour mixture evenly throughout pan. Lay bacon strips horizontally across pan. Bake at 350 degrees until beans have absorbed the majority of the liquid (approximately 45 minutes). *Don't overbake . . . or your beans will dry up! Enjoy!*

## ALFREDO'S MIAMI MARINATED MANGO CHICKEN

4 skinless chicken breasts (4-oz.)
dash pepper, freshly-ground

*Marinade:*       1/4 c. dark rum
                  1/4 c. reduced-sodium soy sauce
                  1/4 c. lime juice

To prepare grill, spray with vegetable oil cooking spray. Stir coals; allow to burn until white ash appears on the surface. To prepare Marinade, warm rum in a small pan over low heat. Remove from heat; ignite with a match. Gently shake the pan back and forth until the flames die out. Add soy sauce and lime juice. Sprinkle chicken with pepper. In a large bowl, marinate chicken, turning pieces to coat evenly. Refrigerate for at least 2 hours. Remove chicken from marinade; place on grill. Brush chicken evenly on each side with marinade. Turn and baste chicken every 3 minutes for 15-20 minutes, or until juices run clear when chicken is pierced. Serve with wild rice.

## ANGEL'S ISLANDER RICE AND BEANS

1 medium onion, finely-chopped
1 T. vegetable oil
1 can red kidney beans or pigeon peas (1-lb.)
1-1/4 c. long-grain rice
1/2 c. coconut milk
1 red hot pepper, seeded and chopped
1 t. thyme leaves
dash of salt and pepper

Saute onions in oil until golden brown. Drain beans; place in a casserole with remaining ingredients. Cover; cook over low heat for 20-30 minutes, or until rice has absorbed all the liquid. Serve steaming hot.

Alfredo and Angel, who is an advertising media coordinator

Alfredo is recognized as one of the NFL's finer blocking tight ends

Angel and Alfredo Roberts own two houses in Florida, operated to provide a home-styled family environment for handicapped children

## SHERRI JO & MICHAEL (MIKE) ERIC SAXON
### * *Number 4* *
### Punter -- 6-3 -- 200

BIRTHDATES: *Mike* -- 7-10-62 (Arcadia, California); *Sherri* -- 9-7-66 (Arcadia, California)

COLLEGES: *Mike* -- San Diego State (Business Management); *Sherri* -- University of Oklahoma

FAVORITE ACADEMIC SUBJECT: *Sherri* -- History

HONORS OR AWARDS: Starred in Baseball and As a Wide Receiver, Defensive Back, and Punter at Arcadia High School; Cowboys' All-Time Leading Punter; Set San Diego State Records for Punting Average in a Game, Season, and Career; Honorable Mention All-America; Holds Record for the Longest Punt in Aztecs History; in 1991, Finished Second in NFC and Tied for Fourth in NFL in Net Punting Average with a 36.8 Mark

HOBBIES & INTERESTS: *Mike* -- Works in the Real Estate Business in Nellie Gale Ranch, California, in the Off-Season; Instructor with Ben Agajanian's Youth Kicking Camps in Long Beach

FAVORITE AUTHOR: *Mike* -- Steven King; *Sherri* -- Danielle Steel

FAVORITE TYPE OF MUSIC: *Mike* -- All Types; *Sherri* -- Country

FAVORITE SPORTS HERO: *Mike* -- Magic Johnson

FAVORITE TV/MOVIE STAR: *Mike* -- Kim Basinger; *Sherri* -- Mel Gibson

CHILDREN & AGES: Erika Leigh - 3 yrs. in January

# MIKE SAXON'S BREAKFAST FOR KING POTATOES

4 large russet potatoes
1 large onion, quartered
1 green pepper, cut into bite-size pieces
3 T. vegetable oil
1/2 t. pepper
1/2 t. season salt

Peel potatoes; cut in bite-size chunks. Boil potatoes until tender but firm. Saute onions and peppers for 3 minutes in oil. Add potatoes; cover, stirring occasionally, for 5 minutes. Remove lid; cook until brown. Serve with eggs, toast, and favorite breakfast meat. (*Hint: Bacon grease adds a great flavor.*)

## SHERRI'S QUICK POPS FOR KIDS

1 can frozen orange juice
1 can frozen cranberry juice
ice cube trays
popsickle sticks

Make juices according to directions on can. Mix juices; pour into ice cube trays. Place sticks in cubes; freeze. *Kids love to make them -- and they're a healthy fun snack to eat!* Try your favorite juices!

Mike Saxon, as the Cowboys' punter for the past seven seasons, walks in the San Diego Zoo with daughter, Erika

Sherri was teaching aerobics at a health club in Arcadia, California, when Mike came in to work out . . . and asked her out that day

Erika Leigh - 3 years old in January

# EMMITT J. SMITH, III
## * *Number 22* *
### Running Back -- 5-9 -- 209

**BIRTHDATE:** 5-15-69 (Pensacola, Florida)

**COLLEGE:** University of Florida (Major -- Therapeutic Recreation)

**GREATEST MOMENT IN SPORTS:** Winning the NFL Leading Rusher Last Year and Winning Two State Championship Games in High School

**GREATEST THRILL ABOUT BEING A PRO ATHLETE:** Being Financial Stable and Seeing So Many of God's Good People

**FAVORITE ACADEMIC SUBJECT:** Math

**HONORS OR AWARDS:** (*JUST TO NAME A FEW*) In 1986 -- All-America Bally Award, All-America High School Football Player of the Year, and National Gatorade Circle of Champions Player of the Year; 1987 -- UPI Freshman of the Year, SEC Player of the Year, and University of Florida MVP; 1988 -- SEC Rookie of the Year and University of Florida MVP; 1989 -- Kodak All-America Football Team and All-American Walter Camp Team; 1990 -- NFL Rookie of the Year and Pro Athlete of the Year for Dallas All Sports Association; 1991 -- Pro Bowl Team, Pensacola Sports Association Athlete of the Year, and NFL Leading Rusher with 1,563 Yards; . . . and Many, Many More

**HOBBIES & INTERESTS:** Golf, Fishing, and Dominos

**FAVORITE AUTHOR:** Alex Haley

**FAVORITE TYPE OF MUSIC:** Rhythm and Blues

**FAVORITE SPORTS HERO:** Tony Dorsett, Walter Payton, and Rocky Blier

**FAVORITE TV/MOVIE STAR:** Bill Cosby

**FAVORITE FOOD:** Barbecue Ribs and Chicken

**PET PEEVE:** Being Interrupted While Engaging in a Conversation and While Eating

**WORST FEAR:** Snakes

## EMMITT'S CHICKEN BARBECUE SAUCE

| | |
|---|---|
| 1/2 c. butter or margarine, melted | 1 t. salt |
| 1/3 c. Worcestershire sauce | 1/2 t. pepper |
| 1/3 c. A-1 sauce | 1 c. water |
| 1/2 c. catsup | 2 cloves garlic, |
| juice of 2 lemons | finely-chopped |
| dash of liquid smoke | 2 chickens |

Combine all ingredients; bring to a boil. Simmer for 20 minutes. Pour generous amount of sauce over chicken before placing on grill. Baste frequently while cooking. Serve remained of sauce over cooked chicken. Can be stored in refrigerator for future use. Makes enough sauce for two chickens.

### MARY E. SMITH'S SHRIMP CREOLE
*(Emmitt's Mother)*

| | |
|---|---|
| 1/4 c. flour | 4 lbs. raw shrimp, peeled and |
| 1/4 c. bacon grease | deveined |
| 1-1/2 c. onions, chopped | 1/2 c. fresh parsley, chopped |
| 1 c. green onions, chopped | 2-3 c. cooked rice |
| 1 c. celery with leaves, chopped | |

1 c. green pepper, chopped
1 clove garlic, minced
1 can tomato paste (6-oz.)
1 can chopped tomatoes, with liquid (16-oz.)
1 can tomato sauce (8-oz.)
1 c. water
5 t. salt
1 t. pepper
1/2 t. red pepper, optional
Tabasco sauce, to taste
2-3 bay leaves
1 t. sugar
1 t. Worcestershire sauce
1 T. lemon juice

In a large, heavy roaster, make a dark brown roux of flour and bacon grease. Add onions, green onions, celery, green pepper, and garlic. Saute until soft (20-30 minutes). Add tomato paste; mix well with vegetables. Add tomatoes and tomato sauce, water, salt, pepper, red pepper, Tabasco sauce, bay leaves, sugar, Worcestershire sauce, and lemon juice. Simmer very slowly for 1 hour (covered), stirring constantly. Add shrimp; cook until done (5-15 minutes). Let sit awhile; much better made the previous day. If made the previous day, reheat — *but do not boil*. Simmer. Freezes well. Add parsley just before serving. Serve over rice. Serves 10 people.

127

Emmitt Smith -- one of the NFL's most talented and dangerous offensive threats

Emmitt became the first Dallas player to ever lead the NFL in rushing -- gaining 1,563 yards in 1991

# VINSON ROBERT SMITH
## *Number 57*
## Linebacker — 6-2 — 237

BIRTHDATE: 7-3-65 (Statesville, North Carolina)

COLLEGE: East Carolina University (B.A. — Communications)

GREATEST MOMENT IN SPORTS: Making the Pros

GREATEST THRILL ABOUT BEING A PRO ATHLETE: Doing Something That I Love, and Being a Part of a Sport That Brings a Lot of Enjoyment to Many People

FAVORITE ACADEMIC SUBJECT: Broadcast Productions

HONORS OR AWARDS: Earned All-State Honors in Both Football and Baseball in High School; Led East Carolina in Tackles Each of His Last Two Seasons; Most Valuable Player (1982-1988) in High School and College

HOBBIES & INTERESTS: Golf, Jogging, Weight Lifting, and Reading

FAVORITE AUTHOR: Richard Wright

FAVORITE TYPE OF MUSIC: Light Jazz

FAVORITE SPORTS HERO: Michael Jordan

FAVORITE TV/MOVIE STAR: Bill Cosby

FAVORITE FOOD: Spicy Fried Chicken

PET PEEVE: Gossip

WORST FEAR: Snakes

CHILDREN & AGES: Jayme - 7-1/2 yrs.

# VINSON'S MACARONI AND CHEESE CASSEROLE

| | |
|---|---|
| 1 pkg. elbow macaroni (8-oz.) | 1 t. pepper |
| 1 T. vegetable oil | 1 t. salt |
| 1/4 c. margarine or butter | 1/2 t. dry mustard |
| 2 T. flour | 1/4 t. paprika |
| 2-1/2 c. milk (2%), or skim milk | |
| sharp Cheddar cheese, grated (16 oz.) | |

Cook macaroni in oil and water until done. Drain; set aside in casserole dish. Preheat oven to 375 degrees. In large saucepan, melt butter over low heat. Add flour gradually, to make smooth paste. Continue to gradually add milk, stirring constantly over heat. Add milk slowly; stir until sauce begins to thicken. Then add more milk (add more or less milk, depending on how bubbly you would like your casserole). Add remaining ingredients, except paprika and enough cheese to sprinkle on top; stir well. Add cheese and paprika on top. Cook at 375 degrees for 25-35 minutes, until slightly brown. Makes 6-8 servings.

## SMITH'S LEMON CHEESECAKE

| | |
|---|---|
| 1 c. sugar | 2 T. lemon juice |
| 2 envelopes unflavored gelatin | 1 t. vanilla |
| 1/4 t. salt | 2 egg whites |
| 1 can evaporated milk (6-oz.) | 1 c. whipping cream, |
| 2 egg yolks, beaten | whipped |
| 1 t. lemon peel, grated | |
| 2 cartons cream-style cottage cheese (12-oz. carton) | |

*Crumb Crust:* 1 c. graham cracker crumbs
1/4 c. sugar
3/4 t. cinnamon
1/4 t. nutmeg
1/4 c. butter

Melt butter; mix with crushed crumbs and other ingredients. Reserve 1/4 c. for garnish. Put remainder on bottom and sides of springform pan (9"). Chill.

In a saucepan, combine 3/4 c. sugar, gelatin, and salt. Stir in cottage cheese, lemon juice, and vanilla; chill. Stir occasionally, until mixture mounds. Beat egg whites to soft peaks. Gradually add 1/4 c. sugar; beat to a stiff peak. Fold into gelatin mixture. Fold in whipped cream. Pour into chilled crust. Sprinkle with remaining crumbs. Chill overnight. Serves 8 people.

Vinson gave a solid performance at the weakside linebacker position in 1991

Last year, Smith made a name for himself as an aggressive hitter and a visible member of the Cowboys' special teams

# MARK MATTHEW STEPNOSKI
## * *Number 53* *
## Center — 6-2 — 269

**BIRTHDATE:** 1-20-67 — Erie, Pennsylvania

**COLLEGE:** University of Pittsburgh (Communications)

**FAVORITE ACADEMIC SUBJECT:** History

**GREATEST MOMENT IN SPORTS:** Starting as a Freshman at the University of Pittsburgh

**GREATEST THRILL ABOUT BEING A PRO ATHLETE:** All the Friendships with People from Different Parts of the Country

**YEARS IN PROFESSIONAL FOOTBALL:** 4th Season

**HONORS OR AWARDS:** Star Football Player at Cathedral Prep High School in Erie, Pennsylvania; Member of National Honor Society; Named High School Football All-America by "USA Today" and "Parade" Magazine in 1984; in 1986, Earned Third-Team All-America Honors and Made Football News Sophomore All-America Team; Won First-Team All-America Honors in 1988; Named an Outland Trophy Finalist and Lombardi Award Semi-Finalist; Two-Time Academic All-America — Kodak All-America and Walter Camp All-America; One of Eleven National Football Foundation and Hall of Fame Scholar-Athletes in 1988

**HOBBIES & INTERESTS:** Music, Working out, Traveling, and Reading; Enjoys Sampling the Cuisine at Many of Dallas' Finest Restaurants

**FAVORITE AUTHOR:** Tom Clancy

**FAVORITE TYPE OF MUSIC:** Classic Rock

**FAVORITE SPORTS HERO:** Mike Webster

**FAVORITE TV/MOVIE STAR:** David Letterman

**FAVORITE FOOD:** "No Distinct Favorite"

## MARK'S MOM'S GERMAN POTATO SALAD

6 potatoes (boiled with skins)    1-1/2 t. salt
6 slices bacon                    1/2 t. celery seed
3/4 c. onion, chopped             1/3 c. vinegar
2 T. flour                        3/4 c. water
1 T. sugar

Peel cooled potatoes; slice. Fry bacon until crisp; crumble over potatoes. Brown onions in bacon grease. Add flour, sugar, salt, pepper, and celery seed; cook until bubbly. Stir in water and vinegar; boil. Pour over potatoes; mix well. Serve warm.

## DAD STEPNOSKI'S FAVORITE BEAN SOUP

2 cans navy beans, *do not drain* (15-oz. can)
2 slices bacon, cut-up
1/4 c. onion, chopped
1/4 c. green pepper, chopped
1/2 c. carrot, chopped
1 clove garlic, minced
1 can diced tomatoes (28-oz.)
1 c. water
1 t. salt
1/4 t. pepper
1/4 t. red pepper
1/2 t. sugar

Fry bacon in large, heavy saucepan until crisp. Drain; set aside. In small amount of drippings, add green pepper, onion, carrot, and garlic; saute for 5 minutes. Add tomatoes, beans, water, salt, pepper, and sugar; simmer for 45 minutes. Add crumbled bacon and parsley; cook 5 minutes longer.

135

Mark -- with Charlie Baumann, former high school teammate, kicker for West Virginia University and New England Patriots

Taken in Boston with former college roommate, Jim Quinn, who is currently a Lieutenant in the Marines, studying to be a pilot

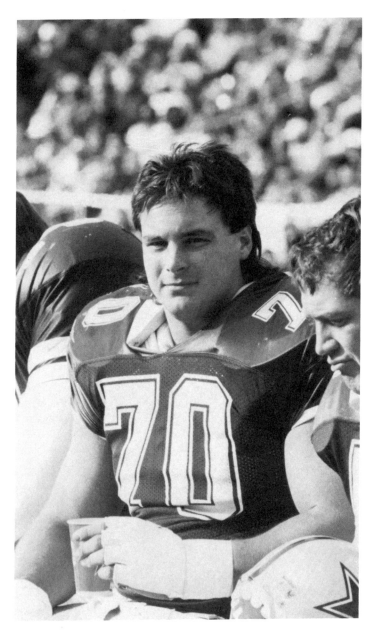

Mark Stepnoski -- one of the key members of the Dallas Cowboys' offensive line

# TONY LEWIS TOLBERT
**\* *Number 92* \***
Defensive End — 6-6 — 265

BIRTHDATE: 12-29-67 (Englewood, New Jersey)

COLLEGE: University of Texas-El Paso (B.A. — Criminal Justice)

GREATEST THRILL ABOUT BEING A PRO ATHLETE: Beating Chicago in Playoff Game

YEARS IN PROFESSIONAL FOOTBALL: 4th Season

HONORS OR AWARDS: Earned All-Conference Recognition at Dwight Morrow High School in Englewood, New Jersey; in 1988, Earned All-Western Athletic Conference and Honorable Mention All-America Honors, after Leading the Miners in Sacks and Tackles for a Loss

FAVORITE AUTHOR: Alex Haley

FAVORITE TYPE OF MUSIC: Rhythm and Blues; Rap

FAVORITE SPORTS HERO: Muhammad Ali

FAVORITE TV/MOVIE STAR: Richard Pryor

FAVORITE FOOD: Chicken and Macaroni

PET PEEVE: People Who Suck up — People Who Follow Someone

WORST FEAR: Getting Bitten by a Snake

## TOLBERT'S FRUIT SALAD

1 large can crushed pineapple, drained
1 small pkg. lemon-flavored Jello
2 pkg. cream cheese, softened (3-oz. pkg.)
1 can dark sweet cherries, drained and cut-up
1/2 c. pecans, chopped
1 carton Cool Whip (8-oz.)

Boil juice from pineapple; add Jello. Let Jello set in refrigerator. After gelling, add nuts, cherries, cream cheese, and Cool Whip; fold in mixture. Refrigerate until serving.


## TONY TOLBERT'S MOM'S CORN CHOWDER

4 slices bacon, cut-up
1 c. onions, chopped
2 c. water
2 c. potatoes, diced
1 large can Pet Milk
1 large can cream-style corn
salt and pepper

Brown cut-up bacon in saucepan over medium heat; add onions. Cook until tender over low heat. Add water and potatoes; cook until potatoes are tender. Add milk and corn. Season salt and pepper, to taste. Heat to serving temperature. *(\* Can add dried flaked veggies.)*

139

Tony, in his first full season as a starter, had the type of performance that should make him one of the defensive stars of the future

Tolbert finished 1991 as the leader in sacks and quarterback pressures, while being the No. 1 tackler of all Dallas' defensive linemen

# PONOLANI (PONO) & MARK PULEMAU (TUI) TUINEI
## * *Number 71* *
## Tackle -- 6-5 -- 298

**BIRTHDATES:** *Mark* -- 3-31-60 (Oceanside, California); *Ponolani (Pono)* -- 2-25-?? (Honolulu, Hawaii)

**COLLEGES:** *Mark* -- U.C.L.A. and University of Hawaii; *Pono* -- Santa Ana College (Liberal Arts)

**GREATEST MOMENT IN SPORTS:** Playing in "Prep Bowl", Hawaii High School Championship (Punahou vs. Waianae)

**GREATEST THRILL ABOUT BEING A PRO ATHLETE:** Being a Teammate with Players, Such as Randy White, Ed Jones, Harvey Martin, and John Dutton

**FAVORITE ACADEMIC SUBJECT:** *Mark* -- ROTC with Lieutenant Colonel William Olds; *Pono* -- Psychology

**WIFE'S OCCUPATION:** Own Entertainment Company Specializing in Laser Karaoke Events [Karaoke Productions] (Sing-a-Long -- Pono Plays a Laser Disc; All You Have to Do Is Sing-a-Long with the Words as They Change Colors on the Screen)

**HONORS OR AWARDS:** *Mark* -- Starred at Punahou High School in Hawaii; Hawaii Prep Lineman of the Year, as a Senior; State Shot Put Champion; All-Star Basketball Player; Defensive Lineman Turned Offensive Lineman Six Years Ago -- One of the Only Players to Play Both Offense and Defense in a NFL Game; Played in More NFL Games (112) Than Any Other Cowboys' Offensive Player

**HOBBIES & INTERESTS:** *Mark* -- Aquariums (Fresh and Salt Water), Golfing, Bowling, Darts, Pool, Basketball, Paddle Tennis, and Cards; *Pono* -- Sing, Dance, and Exercise

**FAVORITE AUTHOR:** *Pono* -- Nana Veary

**FAVORITE TYPE OF MUSIC:** *Mark* -- All Types; *Pono* -- Hawaiian; Rhythm and Blues

**FAVORITE SPORTS HERO:** *Mark* -- Mohammed Ali; *Pono* -- Brother Mike and Uncle Clayton

**FAVORITE TV/MOVIE STAR:** *Mark* -- Al Pacino; *Pono* -- Lucille Ball ("I Love Lucy")

**FAVORITE FOOD:** *Mark* -- Beef Curry, Teri Beef, Chicken Katsu, Two Scoops Rice, Two Scoops Macaroni Salad, and Kim Chee (Hawaiian Mix-Plate Lunch); *Pono* -- Laulau, Lomilomi Salmon, and Poi (Authentic Hawaiian Meal)

**WORST FEAR:** *Mark* -- Fear Itself

142

## TUI'S SEARED PEPPERED AHI

2 Ahi (7-8 oz. each) *[tuna steaks; may use swordfish]*
black peppercorns, crushed (to taste)
salt, to taste
peanut oil

Season Ahi, to taste, with crushed peppercorns and salt. In a large, heavy frypan, heat 1/4" of peanut oil over a high heat; add fish. Sear on both sides to desired degree of doneness. Garnish with tomato wedges and cooked asparagus tips or broccoli florets. (*Note: Mark likes steamed rice with his fish.*)

## PONO'S PORK AND WATERCRESS SOUP

lean pork (2 oz.)
6 c. chicken stock
1/2" fresh ginger, sliced
1-1/2 T. sherry
1/2 bunch watercress, sliced
1 green onion, thinly-sliced
salt, to taste

Combine all ingredients in large pot. Cook until meat is tender. Serve.

143

Pono and Mark Tuinei -- "It's a long story! Let's just say it was love at first bite -- I mean sight!", says Pono

Mark -- starting left tackle for six seasons -- has played in more NFL games than any other Cowboys' offensive player

Pono owns an entertainment company specializing in Laser Karaoke Events (*picture by Mary Ann Changg Photograph)

## ALAN STUART VEINGRAD
### * *Number 76* *
### Offensive Tackle -- 6-5 -- 280

**BIRTHDATES:** *Alan* -- 7-24-63 (Brooklyn, New York); *Marla Reis (Fiancee)* -- 4-16-64 (Miami, Florida)

**COLLEGES:** *Alan* -- East Texas State University (Health and Physical Education); *Marla* -- Florida International University (B.A. -- Psychology); University of Miami (M.S. -- Counseling Psychology); Currently Working on Ph.D. in Counseling Psychology

**GREATEST MOMENT IN SPORTS:** First Start with Dallas Cowboys against His Old Team, the Green Bay Packers, in Which the Cowboys Won

**GREATEST THRILL ABOUT BEING A PRO ATHLETE:** Lockering Next to Kevin Gogan

**HONORS OR AWARDS:** Two-Time All-Lone Star Conference Selection at East Texas State; Four-Year Letterman and Team Captain, as a Junior and Senior; Following Senior Season, Named to Kodak All-America Team, as Well as Earning National Strength and Conditioning All-America Honors

**HOBBIES & INTERESTS:** *Alan* -- Eating, Reading, Fishing, and Goldfish; *Marla* -- Tennis, Reading, and Working out

**FAVORITE AUTHOR:** *Alan* -- John Grisham and Sidney Sheldon; *Marla* -- Mary Higgins-Clark and John Turow

**FAVORITE TYPE OF MUSIC:** *Alan and Marla* -- Rock

**FAVORITE TV/MOVIE STAR:** *Alan* -- Jason Alexander and Robert DeNiro; *Marla* -- Jerry Seinfeld and Harrison Ford

**FAVORITE FOOD:** *Alan* -- Mussels Marinara; *Marla* -- Any Kind of Pasta

**HOW THEY MET:** Met at a Sports Bar ("Coaches") in Miami

**PET PEEVE:** *Alan* -- Dale Hellestrae Getting out of Practice Plays

**WORST FEAR:** *Alan* -- Setting a Goal and Not Reaching It

**PET:** Cat - Ketzel

## BIG AL'S BEER SPUDS

4 medium-size potatoes, cut into bite-size pieces
2 medium white onions, chopped
3/4 can of beer (any kind)
3 cloves garlic, finely-chopped
pepper, to taste
Mrs. Dash, to taste
Lawry's Seasoning Salt, to taste
2 T. butter

Chop onions and cut potatoes into bite-size pieces (not squares). Combine all ingredients in skillet, slowly adding beer as you cook. Cook over low to medium-low heat, stirring frequently. Keep covered while cooking. Cook until potatoes are soft. Makes 2-4 servings.

*You can add your favorite hot sauce.*

## MARLA'S SUN-DRIED TOMATO PESTO

1 lb. uncooked Ziti Rigati
3 c. packed sun-dried tomatoes (*if already in oil, drain*)
1-1/2 c. olive oil
1-1/4 c. Parmesan cheese, grated
1/2 c. fresh parsley leaves
1/2 c. fresh basil
4 medium garlic cloves

Cook Ziti Rigati according to package instructions. Put all ingredients (*except pasta*) in food processor (*with metal blade*). Pulse ingredients several times until coarsely-chopped by turning processor on and off rapidly. Scrape down the work bowl. Process continuously until pesto is smooth. If pesto seems too thick, pulse in a little warm water. Toss with Ziti Rigati the moment the Rigati has been drained. Serves 4-6 people.

Alan caught this dolphin in Costa Rica during this past off-season

Veingrad -- one of the Cowboys' most valuable off-season acquisitions last year -- with fiancee, Marla Reis

Marla is currently a student at the University of Miami, working on a Ph.D. in counseling psychology

## DANA & JAMES MCARTHUR WASHINGTON
### * *Number 37* *
### Safety -- 6-1 -- 203

**BIRTHDATES:** *James* -- 1-10-65 (Los Angeles, California); *Dana* -- 2-16-65 (Whittier, California)

**COLLEGES:** *James* -- U.C.L.A. (B.A. - History); *Dana* -- U.C.L.A. (Major - Communications; Minor - Business)

**FAVORITE ACADEMIC SUBJECT:** *James* -- African-American History; *Dana* -- English

**WIFE'S OCCUPATION:** Freelance Writer-Producer (TV and Radio)

**HONORS OR AWARDS:** *James* -- Earned All-America Honors at Jordan High School in Los Angeles; Four-Year Starter at U.C.L.A.; Earned Honorable Mention All-America Honors, as a Freshman, and Second-Team All-America, as a Sophomore; in Senior Shriner's Bowl and Three Times Rose Bowl Champ Chancellor's Marshall; Named NFC's Defensive Player of the Week; *Dana* -- Chancellor's Marshall and Homecoming Princess

**HOBBIES & INTERESTS:** *James* -- Golfing, Listening to Music, and organized a Student Outreach Program in Los Angeles to Motivate Youngsters to Stay in School and away from Drugs; *Dana* -- Shopping, Reading, and Baking

**FAVORITE AUTHOR:** *Dana* -- Stephen King

**FAVORITE TYPE OF MUSIC:** *James* -- Slow Oldies; *Dana* -- Jazz and Oldies

**FAVORITE SPORTS HERO:** *Dana* -- Husband James

**FAVORITE TV/MOVIE STAR:** *James* -- Al Pacino; *Dana* -- Danny Glover

**FAVORITE FOOD:** *James* -- Italian; *Dana* -- Mexican

**PET PEEVE:** *James* -- People Who Talk the Talk, But Don't Walk the Walk

**CHILDREN & AGES:** Richard Alexander - 1-1/2 yrs.

## JAMES' PAPRIKA POTATOES

| | |
|---|---|
| 1-1/2 lb. potatoes | 1 large tomato, peeled and |
| salt | chopped |
| 2 T. vegetable oil | black pepper, freshly-ground |
| 1 medium onion, sliced | 3 T. dairy sour cream |
| 1 t. paprika | extra paprika, to garnish |
| 1-1/4 c. chicken broth | |
| 1 t. caraway seeds, optional | |

Boil potatoes in salted water until they begin to soften (about 7 minutes). Drain; cut into 1/4" slices. Heat oil in a large saucepan. Cook onion over moderate heat (about 4 minutes), or until just beginning to turn light brown. Add paprika, chicken broth, caraway seeds (if using), tomato, and pepper; stir well. Add potatoes, stirring carefully. Bring slowly to a boil (covered) and simmer for 20-25 minutes. The potatoes should have absorbed most of the liquid. Pour over the dairy sour cream; allow just to heat through. Turn onto a warmed serving dish. Sprinkle with a little extra paprika to garnish. Makes 4 servings.

## DANA'S PEANUT BUTTER COOKIES

| | |
|---|---|
| 1/2 c. margarine | 1 egg (or 2 egg whites, or |
| 1/2 c. peanut butter | egg substitute equal to 1 egg) |
| 1/2 c. granulated sugar | 1/2 t. vanilla |
| 1/2 c. brown sugar | 1 c. flour |
| | 1 t. baking soda |

Cream together margarine and peanut butter. Add white and brown sugar. Stir in egg, vanilla, flour, and baking soda. Shape dough into 1" balls; roll each in granulated sugar (optional). Place on cookie sheet; press with a floured fork. Bake at 375 degrees for 10 minutes. Cool a minute or two before removing from cookie sheet. Makes 4 dozen cookies.

151

The Washingtons met when James presented himself at Dana's job in college -- not budging until she gave him her phone number

What a Cowboy!  Richard Alexander Washington (1-1/2 years old)

Dana & James -- who led all defensive backs & second on the team in tackles with 113 in his first full season as the starting strong safety

# ERIK GEORGE WILLIAMS
**\* *Number 79* \***
Tackle — 6-6 — 321

BIRTHDATE: 9-7-68 (Philadelphia, Pennsylvania)

COLLEGE: Central State University (Physical Education)

GREATEST MOMENT IN SPORTS: College Championship Game

HONORS OR AWARDS: Starred at John Bartram High School; Competed in the Shot Put and Discus in High School; as a Senior, a Small College All-America (1990); in 1990, the Most Valuable Player of the Team; First Offensive Lineman from Central State to Ever Be Selected in the NFL Draft; Took Kodak All-America, Sheridan All-America, and NAIA All-America Honors

HOBBIES & INTERESTS: Cars and Target Shooting

FAVORITE AUTHOR: Alex Haley

FAVORITE TYPE OF MUSIC: Jazz

FAVORITE TV/MOVIE STAR: Denzel Washington

FAVORITE FOOD: Lasagna and Spaghetti

PET PEEVE: Being Interrupted for Autographs While Eating

# ERIK'S GRAHAM CARAMEL FUDGE BROWNIES

1 pkg. Fudge Brownie Mix (21.5-oz.)
1-1/2 c. graham cracker crumbs
1/2 c. sugar
1/2 c. margarine or butter, melted
1 pkg. caramels, unwrapped (14-oz.)
1/3 c. evaporated milk   1 c. pecans, chopped
3/4 c. peanut butter chips  1/4 c. water
3/4 c. semi-sweet chocolate chips 1/4 c. oil
1 egg

Preheat oven to 350 degrees. In medium bowl, combine 1-1/2 c. of Fudge Brownie Mix, graham cracker crumbs, sugar, and melted margarine; mix well. Press mixture into the bottom of an *ungreased* pan (9" x 13"). In medium saucepan, combine caramels and evaporated milk. Cook over medium heat until caramels are melted, stirring constantly. Carefully spread melted caramel mixture over crust. Sprinkle with peanut butter chips, chocolate chips, and 3/4 c. chopped pecans *(reserve remaining 1/4 c. pecans for topping)*. In same medium bowl, combine remaining Fudge Brownie Mix, water, oil, and egg. Beat at least 50 strokes by hand. Carefully spoon batter evenly over pecans. Sprinkle with remaining 1/4 c. pecans. Bake at 350 degrees for 33-38 minutes, or until center is set. Cool completely. Cut into bars. Makes 24 bars.


## WILLIAMS' SEAFOOD SPAGHETTI

box of spaghetti

*Sauce:*   1/2 lb. Italian sausage
     1 can of tiny shrimp
     1/2 can of sliced mushrooms
     1/2 can of diced clams
     1 jar Ragu Spaghetti Sauce
     1/2 lb. hamburger

Boil water in large pot; add spaghetti noodles (cook according to directions on package). Brown sausage and hamburger in skillet. Add shrimp, mushrooms, and clams. Add spaghetti sauce. Heat thoroughly. Place sauce over cooked spaghetti when serving.

Erik held All-Pro defensive end Charles Mann to two tackles and no sacks in the Cowboys win over the Redskins at RFK in 1991

Erik Williams -- a promising performer, who has the size, strength, agility, and toughness to compete at offensive tackle in the NFL

# ROBERT COLE WILLIAMS
**\* *Number 23* \***
Cornerback / Safety – 5-10 – 190

**BIRTHDATE:** 10-2-62 (Galveston, Texas)

**COLLEGE:** Baylor University (Health Education)

**GREATEST MOMENT IN SPORTS:** Touchdown on Special Teams – Houston Game in 1991

**GREATEST THRILL ABOUT BEING A PRO ATHLETE:** Kids Look up to You

**FAVORITE ACADEMIC SUBJECT:** Math

**YEARS IN PROFESSIONAL FOOTBALL:** 6th Season

**HONORS OR AWARDS:** Football and Track Most Valuable Player at Ball High School in Galveston, Texas; Won the District High Hurdles Title as a Senior; Earned a Special Teams Game Ball after Blocking a Punt against Phoenix (1991); Led All Non-Starters in Tackles with 49 and Was the Only Non-Lineman to Record a Sack in 1991

**HOBBIES & INTERESTS:** Fishing, Swimming, Bowling, and Movies

**FAVORITE TYPE OF MUSIC:** All Kinds

**FAVORITE TV/MOVIE STAR:** Martin Lawrence

**FAVORITE FOOD:** Seafood

**CHILDREN & AGES:** Davina - 9 yrs.; and Brandon - 5 yrs.

## ROBERT WILLIAMS' SHRIMP CURRY

1 lb. large shrimp, washed and deveined
2 T. lemon juice      1/2 green pepper, chopped
1/4 t. garlic powder      2 T. curry powder
1/4 t. onion powder (or salt)      1/2 c. water
2 T. vegetable oil      2 c. hot cooked rice
1 medium onion, chopped      raisins

Place shrimp in non-metal container. Combine lemon juice, garlic powder, and onion salt. Heat oil in large skillet. Add onion and green pepper; saute. Stir in curry powder. Add water slowly; simmer for 15 minutes. Add shrimp; cook for 15 minutes. Serve over rice. Garnish with raisins. Serve _hot_!

## ROBERT'S CHOCOLATE-ALMOND-COCONUT PIE

1 prepared 9" one-crust pie shell

_Filling:_      1/3 c. sugar
           1/3 c. cornstarch
           2-1/4 c. milk
           1-1/2 c. semi-sweet chocolate chips
           1 to 1-1/2 t. almond extract
           1-1/2 c. coconut
           1/2 c. cream of coconut
           1 c. whipping cream
           3 T. powdered sugar
           1/2 c. almonds, sliced

Prepare pie crust according to package directions; bake until lightly-browned. Cool completely. In medium saucepan, combine sugar and cornstarch; blend well. Stir in milk; cook over medium heat until mixture thickens and boils (12-15 min.), stirring constantly. Remove from heat. Add chocolate chips and almond extract; stir until chips are melted and mixture is smooth. Cover surface of chocolate mixture with plastic wrap. Refrigerate 45-60 minutes, or until mixture reaches room temperature. In medium bowl, combine coconut and cream of coconut; mix well. Refrigerate for 15 minutes. In small bowl, combine whipping cream and powdered sugar; beat until soft peaks form. Fold 1/2 c. whipped cream into cooled chocolate mixture; blend well. Spoon 1/2 of chocolate mixture into crust-lined pan. Carefully spoon chilled coconut mixture over chocolate mixture. Spread remaining chocolate mixture over coconut mixture. Garnish with remaining whipped cream; sprinkle with almonds. Refrigerature until serving time. Store in refrigerator. Makes 8-10 servings.

Robert speaks often at public schools, warning students of the dangers of drug use

Robert's other charitable activities include the March of Dimes, Boys and Girls Clubs, and Clown Ministries to children's hospitals

Robert Williams -- one of the most versatile players on the defensive side of the ball

# ROOKIES & RECENTLY ACQUIRED PLAYERS

## MICHAEL K. BEASLEY
*Rookie Free Agent*
Running Back -- 5-10 -- 203

BIRTHDATE: 5-27-69 (Pottstown, Pennsylvania)

COLLEGE: Maryland and West Virginia University

GREATEST MOMENT IN SPORTS: Being Called by the Dallas Cowboys

GREATEST THRILL ABOUT BEING A PRO ATHLETE: Wearing the Helmet with the Star!

FAVORITE ACADEMIC SUBJECT: Philosophy

HONORS OR AWARDS: Starred at Owen J. Roberts High School in Pottstown; Toyota Leadership Award; as a Freshman at Maryland, Finished Second in ACC with a 21.1 Yard Kickoff Return Average; Led Team in Rushing, as a Junior at Maryland; Posted Longest Run of the Season, as a Senior

HOBBIES & INTERESTS: Music and Reading (Poetry, History, and Philosophy)

FAVORITE AUTHOR: Renee Descartes

FAVORITE TYPE OF MUSIC: Jazz (Loves Prince)

FAVORITE SPORTS HERO: Walter Payton

FAVORITE TV/MOVIE STAR: Bill Cosby

FAVORITE FOOD: Italian

PET PEEVE: People Who Don't Believe in the Power of the Lord

Michael is thrilled to wear the helmet with the star

## MICHAEL BEASLEY'S GINGERBREAD

2-1/2 c. flour
1 c. sugar
1 c. Wesson Oil
1 c. molasses
1 T. ginger
1 t. cinnamon
1/2 t. cloves
2 t. baking soda
1 t. salt
1 c. very hot water
2 eggs, beaten

Measure flour; add spices and salt. Set aside in a bowl. In another large bowl, mix sugar and Wesson Oil; beat until well-mixed. Boil water; add baking soda to hot water. Add flour mixture alternately to sugar and Wesson Oil; mix with the hot water. Mix well. Add beaten eggs; mix well. Pour into a greased 9" x 12" baking pan. Bake at 350 degrees for 30-35 minutes. Do not overcook. Test with cake tester.

## BEASLEY'S FRIED YELLOW SQUASH

2 large yellow squash, chopped (do not peel skin)
2 medium yellow onions, peeled and thinly-sliced
1 large green pepper, chopped
2 t. olive oil, or vegetable oil

Heat olive oil in large frying pan. Add all of chopped vegetables to hot frying oil. Turn heat to low setting. Season vegetables with salt and pepper. Place lid on frying pan. Cook until vegetables are to desired tenderness, stirring occasionally.

GREG BRIGGS
* *Number 42* *
Safety -- 6-3 -- 212

BIRTHDATE: 10-19-68 (Meadville, Mississippi)

COLLEGE: Texas Southern University

YEARS IN PROFESSIONAL FOOTBALL: 1991 Draft Choice

HONORS OR AWARDS: All-District Basketball Player, as a Senior, at Franklin County High School in Meadville; Received Basketball Scholarship to Lincoln Junior College, Playing in 1987 and 1988; Joined the Football Team in 1989, Earning JUCO All-State Honors as a Safety for the Wolves; Third Texas Southern Player Ever Drafted by the Cowboys

# GREG'S SOUTHERN SOUR CREAM COOKIES

| | |
|---|---|
| 1/3 c. shortening | 1/2 c. commercial sour cream |
| 2/3 c. sugar | 1/2 c. walnuts, chopped |
| 1 egg | sugar |
| 1-3/4 c. all-purpose flour | 2 T. sugar |
| 1 t. baking powder | 1/2 t. ground cinnamon |
| 1/4 t. baking soda | |
| 1/2 t. salt | |

Combine shortening and 2/3 c. sugar in a large mixing bowl; beat well. Add egg; beat well. Combine flour, baking powder, baking soda, and salt; add to creamed mixture alternately with sour cream -- beginning and ending with flour mixture. Stir in walnuts. Drop dough by heaping teaspoon- fuls onto lightly-greased cookie sheets. Dip bottom of a glass in water; dip in sugar, and gently press each cookie until 2" in diameter. Combine 2 T. sugar and cinnamon; lightly sprinkle over cookies. Bake at 400 degrees for 10-12 minutes; cook on wire racks. Makes 3-1/2 dozen.

## BRIGGS' COMPANY PORK CHOPS

| | |
|---|---|
| 1/2 c. all-purpose flour | 2 T. butter or margarine |
| 1/2 t. dried whole thyme | 2 T. vegetable oil |
| 1/2 t. salt | 1 c. dry vermouth |
| 1/4 t. pepper | 1/2 lb. fresh mushrooms, sliced |
| 6 pork chops (1" thick) | 6 slices Swiss cheese (1 oz.) |

Combine first 4 ingredients. Dredge pork chops in flour mixture. Heat butter and oil in an electric skillet over medium heat. Brown pork chops on both sides; drain off pan drippings. Add vermouth; cover and reduce heat. Simmer for 25 minutes. Add mushrooms; cover and simmer an additional 20 minutes. Turn off heat; top each pork chop with a slice of cheese. Cover; let stand until cheese melts. Serves 6 people.

Greg Briggs -- a big safety from Texas Southern with excellent speed and hitting ability

# ROBIN & FRANK EDGAR CORNISH
## * *Number 68* *
### Center/Guard -- 6-4 -- 295

**BIRTHDATES:** *Frank* -- 9-24-67 (Chicago, Illinois); *Robin Skyles Blake* -- 9-17-69 (Chicago, Illinois)

**COLLEGES:** *Frank* -- U.C.L.A. (History); *Robin* -- Occidental College (Psychology)

**GREATEST MOMENT IN SPORTS:** Starting Center in Rookie Season

**YEARS IN PROFESSIONAL FOOTBALL:** San Diego Chargers -- 2 Yrs.; Dallas Cowboys -- 1st Season

**FAVORITE ACADEMIC SUBJECT:** *Frank* -- African-American History; *Robin* -- Social Psychology and Race/Ethnic Relations

**WIFE'S OCCUPATION:** Special Education Teacher

**HONORS OR AWARDS:** *Frank* -- One of the Most Highly-Recruited Linemen in the Country in High School; Earned Three Letters as a Two-Way Tackle in High School; Earned First-Team All-America Recognition from the Football News; All-PAC 10 Second-Team Selection Following Senior Year; Finished Career Ranked Fourth in the School's Weight Room Record Book with a Three Lift (Bench, Squat, and Clean) Total of 1,253 Pounds

**HOBBIES & INTERESTS:** *Frank* -- Hunting and Reading Books; *Robin* -- Crocheting, Singing, and Designing Jewelry

**FAVORITE AUTHOR:** *Frank* -- James Baldwin; *Robin* -- Maya Angelou

**FAVORITE TYPE OF MUSIC:** *Frank* -- Rhythm and Blues; *Robin* -- Gospel

**FAVORITE SPORTS HERO:** *Frank* -- Earl Campbell; *Robin* -- Wilma Rudolph

**FAVORITE TV/MOVIE STAR:** *Frank* -- Jasmine Guy; *Robin* -- Wesley Snipes

**FAVORITE FOOD:** *Frank* -- Soul Food; *Robin* -- Shrimp

Cornish and Aikman made up the starting center/quarterback combination for two complete seasons in 1987 and 1988 at U.C.L.A.

Robin and Frank are both from Chicago

# FRANK'S SOUTHERN CHOCOLATE POUND CAKE

| | |
|---|---|
| 1/2 c. Crisco shortening | 1/2 c. cocoa |
| 1 c. butter or margarine | 1 t. baking powder |
| 3 c. sugar | 1/4 t. salt |
| 5 eggs | 1 c. milk |
| 3 c. flour | 3/4 t. vanilla |

Preheat oven to 325 degrees. Cream together Crisco, butter, and sugar. Add eggs, one at a time, beating well after each addition. Sift flour; measure after sifting. Sift together dry ingredients; Sift several times until cocoa is well-blended with flour. Add dry ingredients and milk alternately to sugar-egg mixture. Add vanilla; mix well. Bake in a tube or Bundt pan at 325 degrees for 1 hour and 45 minutes. Remove cake from oven; let sit in the pan for 10 minutes before removing to a rack to cool completely.

## JEANETTE'S SEAFOOD CASSEROLE

| | |
|---|---|
| 1 pkg. imitation crab meat | 1 pkg. Monterrey Jack cheese |
| 1 red pepper, chopped | 1 egg |
| 1 green pepper, chopped | 1/3 c. milk |
| 1 onion, chopped | 1 can crescent rolls (Pillsbury) |
| 1 T. butter | |

Chop up red pepper, green pepper, and onion; set aside. Cut imitation crab meat into small pieces. Melt butter; saute peppers, onion, and crab meat. Season to taste. Remove crab mixture from heat. Add egg, milk, and cheese; mix together. In an ungreased casserole dish, lay four crescents on the bottom of the dish. Put mixture in the dish. Place remaining four crescents on top. In 375-degree oven, bake casserole until golden brown. (*Can use lobster or shrimp, in place of crab meat, according to your preference!*)

# TIM DANIEL
*\* Number 3 \**
Wide Receiver -- 5-11 -- 192

**BIRTHDATE:** 9-14-69 (Atlanta, Georgia)

**COLLEGE:** Florida A & M (Journalism)

**YEARS IN PROFESSIONAL FOOTBALL:** 1991 Draft Choice

**HONORS OR AWARDS:** All-Conference and All-County Selection in Both Football and Track at Benjamin Mays High School in Atlanta, Georgia; Earned Honorable Mention All-MEAC Selection in 1990; Big Play Man with Career Receiving Average of 21.2 Yards; Had 61 Catches and 7 Touchdown Receptions in 3 Years as a Starter; Only Florida A & M Player Taken in 1991 Draft; First Player Drafted by Dallas from Florida A & M since 1966

## TIM'S OLD SOUTH BARBECUED CHICKEN

1 broiler-fryer, cut up (2-1/2 to 3 lb.)
salt
1/2 c. all-purpose flour
1/3 c. vegetable oil
1 medium onion, diced
1/2 c. celery, chopped
1 c. catsup
1 c. water
1/4 c. lemon juice
3 T. Worcestershire sauce
2 T. brown sugar
2 T. vinegar
1 small hot pepper
hot cooked rice or noodles

Sprinkle chicken with salt. Dredge chicken in flour; brown in hot oil in a Dutch oven. Remove chicken from Dutch oven; drain off excess oil. Combine remaining ingredients (except rice) in Dutch oven; add chicken. Cover; bake at 350 degrees for 1 hour. Remove hot pepper; discard. Serve over rice or noodles. Makes 4 servings.

## DANIEL'S BLUEBERRY-OATMEAL BREAD

2 c. all-purpose flour
1 c. quick-cooking oats, uncooked
1/2 c. sugar
1 T. baking powder
1/2 t. baking soda
1/2 t. salt
1/2 t. ground cinnamon
1/4 c. plus 2 T. butter or margarine, softened
2 eggs, slightly-beaten
1 c. milk
1/4 c. light corn syrup
1 c. fresh blueberries

Combine first 7 ingredients in a large mixing bowl. Cut in butter with a pastry blender until mixture resembles coarse meal. Combine eggs, milk, and corn syrup; mix well. Add to the dry ingredients, stirring just until moistened. Fold in blueberries. Pour batter into a greased and floured loaf pan (9" x 5" x 3"); bake at 350 degrees for 1 hour and 10 minutes, or until a wooden pick inserted in center comes out clean. Cool loaf in pan for 10 minutes; remove from pan and cool completely on a wire rack. Makes 1 loaf.

# LIN ELLIOTT
*\* Number 2 \**
Kicker -- 6-0 -- 182

**BIRTHDATE:** 11-11-68 (Euless, Texas)

**COLLEGE:** Texas Tech University (Finance)

**YEARS IN PROFESSIONAL FOOTBALL:** Rookie

**GREATEST MOMENT IN SPORTS:** Any Game-Winning Field Goals

**GREATEST THRILL ABOUT BEING A PRO PLAYER:** Playing for the Dallas Cowboys

**FAVORITE ACADEMIC SUBJECT:** Finance

**HONORS OR AWARDS:** Starred at Waco, Texas, High School, as a Four-Time All-District Selection in Soccer; All-Southwest Conference Selection, as a Senior; Holds Texas Tech University's All-Time Career Record for Kick Scoring (220 Points), Conversions (100), and Consecutive Extra Points (85)

**HOBBIES & INTERESTS:** Any Outdoor Activities

**FAVORITE AUTHOR:** Joseph Wambaugh

**FAVORITE TYPE OF MUSIC:** Country

**FAVORITE SPORTS HERO:** Roger Staubach

**FAVORITE TV/MOVIE STAR:** John Wayne

**FAVORITE FOOD:** Chicken Tetrazinni

**PET PEEVE:** Losing to Saxon in Anything

**WORST FEAR:** Losing the Rest of My Hair

## LIN'S CHICKEN SPAGHETTI

1 chicken, cooked and cut-up
1 pkg. cut spaghetti
1 medium onion, chopped
1 green pepper, chopped
2-3 stalks celery, chopped
1/2 c. butter
1 can cream of chicken soup
1 c. chicken broth
2 T. pimento
American or Velveeta cheese (8 oz.)
1/2 t. garlic

Saute onions, peppers, and celery in butter. Cook spaghetti according to directions on package; drain. Mix spaghetti, soup, and all other ingredients together. Add sauteed onions, peppers, and celery to mixture. Bake at 350 degrees for 25 minutes, or until heated thoroughly.

## ELLIOTT'S BUTTER SUGAR COOKIES

1 c. butter
1 c. sugar
1/2 t. vanilla
1 egg
2 c. flour
1/2 t. soda
1/2 t. cream of tartar

Cream butter and sugar together; add vanilla and egg. Add sifted dry ingredients; mix thoroughly. Chill dough. Place on cookie sheet in small balls; flatten with fork dipped in sugar, making sure each cookie is sprinkled with sugar. Bake at 350 degrees until edge of cookie just begins to turn golden (about 10 minutes). Makes 2 dozen cookies.

Lin, for his college career, hit 100-of-101 extra points and 40-of-62 field goals

# EDITH RENEE & MELVIN C. EVANS
## * *Number 60* *
### Guard / Tackle -- 6-2 -- 303

**BIRTHDATES:** *Melvin* -- 1-29-69 (Jacksonville, Florida); *Edith Renee Moore* -- 9-23-?? (Houston, Texas)

**COLLEGES:** *Melvin* -- Garden City College (Kansas) and Texas Southern University (Associate Degree: Art); *Edith Renee* -- Texas Southern University (B.S. -- Biology/Chemistry)

**YEARS IN PROFESSIONAL FOOTBALL:** Rookie Free Agent

**GREATEST MOMENT IN SPORTS:** State Championship in High School

**GREATEST THRILL ABOUT BEING A PRO ATHLETE:** Playing in the NFL with Great Athletes

**FAVORITE ACADEMIC SUBJECT:** *Melvin* -- Math; *Edith Renee* -- Science

**WIFE'S OCCUPATION:** Middle School Science Teacher

**HONORS OR AWARDS:** *Melvin* -- All-Conference Selection at Peter Quinn High School in Trenton, New Jersey; All-Southwestern Athletic Conference Selection at Right Guard; Earned All-America Honors as an Offensive Guard and Tackle at Garden City Community College; *Edith Renee* -- "Who's Who in America"; Teacher of the Month; and Teacher of the Year

**HOBBIES & INTERESTS:** *Melvin* -- Watching NFL Highlight Films

**FAVORITE AUTHOR:** *Melvin and Edith Renee* -- Alice Walker

**FAVORITE TYPE OF MUSIC:** *Melvin* -- Rap; *Edith Renee* -- Rhythm and Blues

**FAVORITE SPORTS HERO:** *Melvin* -- Jim Brown; *Edith Renee* -- Husband Melvin

**FAVORITE TV/MOVIE STAR:** *Melvin* -- Hally Berry; *Edith Renee* -- Eddie Murphy

**HOW THEY MET:** Met at a Laundry Mat, Shopping Mall, Club, and Grocery Store -- All in One Week's Time -- Kept Running into Each Other and the Relationship Grew from Those Meetings

**CHILDREN & AGES:** Melvin Patrick - 3 mon.

"Big" Mel and "Little" Mel

Melvin and Edith Renee with Melvin Patrick Evans

## MELVIN EVANS' OLD-FASHIONED POUND CAKE

3-1/4 c. flour
3 c. sugar
1 t. baking powder
5 eggs
1/2 c. Crisco
1/2 lb. butter
1 c. milk
1 t. vanilla

Mix dry ingredients together (flour and baking powder). Fold in the butter, sugar, and Crisco. Add eggs, milk, and flavoring. Place batter in loaf pan. Bake at 325 degrees for about 1 hour.

## EDITH RENEE'S FRUIT COTTAGE CHEESE SALAD

3 c. cream-style cottage cheese
1 qt. Cool Whip, slightly-thawed
2 pkgs. orange-flavored Jello (3-oz. pkg.)
1 small can Mandarin oranges, drained
1 small can pineapple chunks, drained

Combine all the ingredients in a large bowl. Blend well. Chill and serve.

## PATT EVANS
*Rookie Free Agent*
Tight End -- 6-6 -- 261


BIRTHDATE: 3-14-69 (Pittsburgh, Pennsylvania)

COLLEGE: University of Minnesota (Human Relationships)

GREATEST MOMENT IN SPORTS: Playing and Having Fun

GREATEST THRILL ABOUT BEING A PRO ATHLETE: An Opportunity to Continue Playing a Game I Love

HONORS OR AWARDS: Three-Time All-Conference Selection at Tight End, Defensive End, and Place Kicker in High School; Earned Honorable Mention All-America and First-Team All-Big 10 Honors in 1991

FAVORITE ACADEMIC SUBJECT: Family / Youth Studies

FAVORITE AUTHOR: Charles Law (6th Grade English Teacher - Great Poet!)

FAVORITE TYPE OF MUSIC: Country

FAVORITE SPORTS HERO: My Father

FAVORITE TV/MOVIE STAR: John Candy

FAVORITE FOOD: Pizza and Hamburgers

PET PEEVE: Prejudice

WORST FEAR: Not Giving Everything I Have

## PATT'S PASTA PRIMAVERA

2 lbs. fresh Fettucine noodles
1 head fresh broccoli
6 fresh carrots
1/2 to 1 c. snow peas
mushrooms, thickly-sliced
1 fresh scallions, thinly-sliced

1 can chicken broth
1 pt. heavy cream
1 stick butter
1 c. Parmesan cheese, grated

Parboil broccoli, carrots, and snow peas for 1 minute (until color is bright). Saute scallions and mushrooms until tender with one full stick of butter. Set all aside. (*Note: Chopped shrimp or chicken can be added, if you so choose.*) Boil noodles according to directions on package. Put noodles in large container. Add can chicken broth; mix thoroughly. Add butter, mushrooms, and onions; mix thoroughly. Add pint of heavy cream; mix thoroughly. Add grated cheese, to taste. Add remaining vegetables; mix again. Serves 8 people.

## EVANS' HOT SAUSAGE SANDWICHES

3 lbs. Italian hot sausage
2 medium onions, thickly-sliced
1 green pepper, thickly-sliced
2 T. dried red pepper flakes

1 can tomato paste (18-oz.)

Cut hot sausage in pieces (to equal 4 per lb.). Layer tomato paste, sausage, peppers, onions; repeat layering until all ingredients are in the casserole. Sprinkle hot red pepper in each layer. Add water to cover enough to reach the top of the last layer. Cover; cook at 325 degrees for 2 hours. Cover may be removed last half-hour to allow sauce to thicken. Stir once or twice each hour. Adjust pepper flakes for desired spicy flavor. Serves 16 sandwiches.

## PATT EVANS' CRUNCHY JUMBLES

1-1/4 c. flour
1/2 t. baking soda
1/4 t. salt
1/2 c. margarine
1 pkg. chocolate chips (6-oz.)

1 c. sugar
1 egg
1 t. vanilla
2 c. Rice Krispies

Sift flour, baking soda, and salt together. Beat margarine, sugar, egg, and vanilla until fluffy. Sift in dry ingredients. Add Rice Krispies and chocolate chips, mixing with wooden spoon. Drop by teaspoon onto greased cookie sheet. Bake at 350 degrees for 12 minutes. Makes 3 dozen cookies. Recipe doubles easily.

Patt with the Evans Family

## STACY & MELVIN FOSTER
*Rookie Free Agent*
Linebacker — 6-1 — 243

**BIRTHDATES:** *Melvin* — 12-23-66 (Houston, Texas); *Stacy* — 1-25-69 (Waterloo, Iowa)

**COLLEGES:** *Melvin* — University of Iowa (General Studies); *Stacy* — University of Iowa

**GREATEST THRILL ABOUT BEING A PRO ATHLETE:** Being Paid for Something I Love

**FAVORITE ACADEMIC SUBJECT:** *Melvin* — Marriage and Family Interaction; *Stacy* — Nursing Studies

**WIFE'S OCCUPATION:** Housewife and Mother

**HONORS OR AWARDS:** *Melvin* — Two-Time All-State Pick at Yates High School, Which Went Undefeated on Its Way to the State 5-A Title, as a Senior; Parade Magazine Rated Foster the Top Linebacker in the Country in 1985; Led Iowa in Tackles in 1989 and 1990; AP and UPI All-Big Ten in 1990; Second-Team All-America (1990); *Stacy* — State of Iowa Scholar in 1987

**FAVORITE AUTHOR:** *Melvin* — Alex Haley; *Stacy* — LaVyrle Spencer

**FAVORITE TYPE OF MUSIC:** *Melvin* — Rap, Pop, and Some Country; *Stacy* — Rhythm and Blues

**FAVORITE SPORTS HERO:** *Stacy* — Michael Jordan

**FAVORITE TV/MOVIE STAR:** *Melvin* — Bill Cosby; *Stacy* — Martin Lawrence

**FAVORITE FOOD:** *Melvin* — Fried Chicken, Hamburgers, and French Fries; *Stacy* — Pizza

**WHERE THEY MET:** Lived in the Same Dormitory in College

**PET PEEVE:** *Melvin* — People Asking for a Autograph While with My Family

**WORST FEAR:** *Melvin* — Waking up and Having the Sport I Love Taken from Me

**CHILDREN & AGES:** Michael Alexander - 8 mon.

Melvin and Stacey met while attending the University of Iowa

Michael Alexander Foster -- born January 6, 1992

# MELVIN'S MOM'S ENCHILADA CASSEROLE

1 to 1-1/2 lbs. lean ground beef
1 can chili (32-oz., or more)
1 pkg. enchilada mix
1 pkg. half-moon Cheddar cheese
1 T. McCormick Season-All Salt
1 T. McCormick Chili Powder
1 T. McCormick Garlic Powder
2 small bags of Doritos (Nacho Cheese)

Fry hamburger; drain off fat. Add seasonings to meat while frying. After fat is drained off, add chili, enchilada mix, and 1 chili can full of water. Let mixture simmer for about 5-10 minutes. Grate cheese. In 9" x 13" pan, layer Doritos, cheese, and meat mixture, ending with Doritos and cheese on top. Bake at 350 degrees for 20-25 minutes, or until cheese is melted.

## STACY'S BUSTER BAR DESSERT

1 pkg. Oreo cookies, crushed (15-oz.)
1/4 c. margarine
1/2 gal. vanilla ice cream
1 can Spanish peanuts
1 pt. jar Mrs. Richardson's Hot Fudge Sauce

Mix cookies and margarine together. Press mixture into 9" x 13" pan. Layer ice cream, then peanuts. Freeze until solid. Spread hot fudge sauce on top; refreeze. Serves 12-15 people.

## JASON GARRETT
*Newly-Acquired Player*
Quarterback -- 6-2 -- 195

BIRTHDATE: 3-28-66 (Abington, Pennsylvania)

COLLEGE: Princeton (B.A. -- History)

YEARS IN PROFESSIONAL FOOTBALL: New Orleans Saints (Rookie) - 1 Yr.; Canadian Football League - 1 Yr.; Dallas Cowboys - 1st Season

GREATEST MOMENT IN SPORTS: Come-from-Behind Win over Lehigh (16-15) While at Princeton

GREATEST THRILL ABOUT BEING A PRO ATHLETE: Play with and against Great Players

FAVORITE ACADEMIC SUBJECT: Recent American History

HONORS OR AWARDS: Named the Ivy League Player of the Year in 1988

FAVORITE AUTHOR: J. D. Salinger

FAVORITE TYPE OF MUSIC: Folk Rock and Blues Rock

FAVORITE SPORTS HERO: Brian Sipe

FAVORITE TV/MOVIE STAR: Robert Duvall

FAVORITE FOOD: Pasta

PET PEEVE: Stuck in Traffic

WORST FEAR: Loss of Good Health

## GARRETT'S ORIENTAL SHRIMP

| | |
|---|---|
| 1 lb. shrimp | 2 small or 1 large onion, sliced |
| 1 green pepper, julienned | 1/2 bunch broccoli, cut up |
| 1 red pepper, julienned | 1 stalk bok-choi, sliced |
| 1 yellow pepper, julienned | 2-3 lemons, squeezed |
| 1/2 bunch fresh dill | olive oil |
| 2-3 T. garlic, minced | clam juice |
| Angel Hair pasta | salt and white pepper, to taste |

Put olive oil in frying pan. Begin cooking shrimp in oil; cook until half-done. Add peppers, garlic, onion, bok-choi, and broccoli; saute. Add lemons and clam juice; simmer. Add dill and salt and pepper, to taste. Place over Angel Hair pasta (cook according to directions on package). Makes 4 servings.

## JASON'S LINGUINE AND CREAMY WHITE CLAM SAUCE

| | |
|---|---|
| 2 T. garlic, chopped | 1 pt. heavy cream |
| 1-1/2 T. ginger, chopped | Parmesan cheese, to taste |
| 2-3 cans clams, chopped | 2-3 T. olive oil |
| clam juice (5 oz. -- for flavor) | |
| 3-4 T. white wine (for flavor) | |
| 1-1/2 boxes Linguine | |

Put olive oil in large frying pan. Saute chopped garlic and ginger together in oil. Add clams; heat. Glaze pan with white wine; reduce heat. Add clam juice; reduce heat. Add heavy cream; reduce heat until consistency becomes a thicker sauce. If desired, add Parmesan cheese. Ladle sauce over cooked Linguine (cook according to directions on package). Makes 4 servings.

## JASON GARRETT'S FRUIT SHAKE

| | |
|---|---|
| 2 bananas | orange juice (4 oz.) |
| 8-10 strawberries | ice |

Place bananas, strawberries, orange juice, and lots of ice in blender. Blend for approximately 1 minute, or until ingredients are completely mixed and you've achieved desired consistency.

188

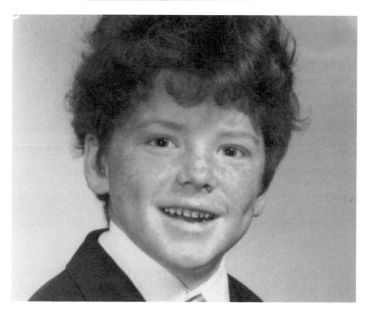

Jason Garrett in grade school

Jason with two brothers, Todd and John

# TAMARA (TAMMY) & CHAD HENNINGS
## * *Number 95* *
### Defensive End — 6-6 — 272

BIRTHDATES: *Chad* — 10-20-65 (Cedar Rapids, Iowa); *Tamara (Tammy)* — 12-11-66 (Salida, Colorado)

COLLEGES: *Chad* — United States Air Force Academy (B.S. — Financial Management); *Tammy* — Americana Beauty Academy (Trade School)

YEARS IN PROFESSIONAL FOOTBALL: Rookie

GREATEST MOMENT IN SPORTS: First Sack in College

GREATEST THRILL ABOUT BEING A PRO ATHLETE: Finally Being with the Cowboys after 4 Years

FAVORITE ACADEMIC SUBJECT: *Chad* — Math and Science; *Tammy* — English Literature

HONORS OR AWARDS: Two-Time All-State Football Player and State-Champion Wrestler in High School; in 1985, Earned Honorable Mention All-America and Second-Team All-WAC Honors as a Sophomore; in 1986, Earned First-Team All-WAC Recognition While Named Honorable Mention All-America; Two-Time Academic All-America NCAA Scholarship Winner; Japan Bowl MVP; 1987 Western Athletic Conference Defensive Player of the Year Honors; 1987 All-America and Outland Trophy Winner

HOBBIES & INTEREST: *Chad* — Watching Movies, Flying, and Reading; *Tammy* — Golf, Volleyball, Reading, Working out, Spending Time with Her Honey

FAVORITE AUTHOR: *Chad* — Tom Clancy; *Tammy* — Ann Rice

FAVORITE TYPE OF MUSIC: *Chad* — Classic Rock; *Tammy* — All Types (Especially Jazz and Country)

FAVORITE SPORTS HERO: *Chad* — Dan Gable; *Tammy* — Michael Jordan

FAVORITE TV/MOVIE STAR: *Chad* — John Wayne; *Tammy* — Marilyn Monroe

FAVORITE FOOD: *Chad* — Pizza; *Tammy* — Mexican

The Hennings met in Colorado Springs through mutual friends in 1988; married in 1990 at the Air Force Academy

Tammy and Chad in England in 1991, where he was home from Turkey deployment after serving a four-year military commitment

## CHAD'S COUNTRY RIBS

ribs (approximately 2 lbs. per person)

Place ribs in large pan; cover with water. Bring to a boil; simmer for 45 minutes. Drain. Then brown ribs, on both sides, on grill.

*Barbecue Sauce:* 1 c. ketchup
1-1/3 c. sugar
8 T. Worcestershire sauce
2 T. dry mustard

Stir all ingredients together in saucepan. Bring to a boil; simmer for 15 minutes.

Dip ribs in Barbecue Sauce; place on grill again to seal in sauce. *Serve with Iowa sweet corn and potatoes!*

## TAMMY'S CHICKEN AND SOUR CREAM ENCHILADAS

2 c. cooked and chopped chicken breast
2 cloves garlic, minced
1/2 c. onion, chopped
1/2 c. green pepper, chopped
2 T. oil or butter
2 T. flour
2 c. chicken broth (*I use bouillon*)
1 can mild green chilis, chopped
2 pt. sour cream
4 c. Monterrey Jack cheese, grated
paprika
salt and pepper
tortillas

Cook and chop chicken; set aside. Saute garlic, onion, and peppers in 2 T. oil or butter until tender. Stir in flour; cook for 1 minute. Add chicken broth; cook until thickened. Add chilis; reduce heat. Add sour cream and 1 c. cheese; stir until smooth. Dip each tortilla in sauce. Place a large spoonful of chicken, sauce, and cheese in center of tortilla. Roll up; place in ungreased baking pan. Pour remaining sauce over all. Sprinkle remaining cheese on top. Sprinkle paprika and pepper on top. Bake at 350 degrees for 25-30 minutes, or until cheese is slightly browned. Serve avocado, lettuce, tomato, and salsa on top! Makes about 6. (*This is our favorite! I make it faithfully about once a week.*)

192

# CLAYTON A. HOLMES
*Number 47*
Cornerback — 5-10 — 181

**BIRTHDATES:** *Clayton* — 8-23-69 (Florence, South Carolina); *Lisa (Fiancee)* — 3-21-69 (Lenoir City, Tennessee)

**COLLEGES:** *Clayton* — North Greenville Junior College and Carson-Newman College (Major: Management); *Lisa* — Carson-Newman College (Double Major: Psychology and Human Services)

**YEARS IN PROFESSIONAL FOOTBALL:** 1991 Draft Choice

**GREATEST MOMENT IN SPORTS:** Beating the #1 High School in South Carolina (14-13) to Go to the Playoffs (Clayton Made Both Touchdowns and Both Extra Points)

**GREATEST THRILL ABOUT BEING A PRO ATHLETE:** Being Successful

**FAVORITE ACADEMIC SUBJECT:** *Lisa* — Child Development Classes

**FIANCEE'S OCCUPATION:** Soon-to-Be Housewife and Mother

**HONORS OR AWARDS:** *Clayton* — All-Conference Honors as a Quarterback and Defensive Back in High School; Set the South Carolina State Record in the Long Jump; Junior College All-America Quarterback at North Greenville; Two-Time NAIA All-America at Cornerback at Carson-Newman; South Atlantic Conference's Defensive Player of the Year, as a Senior

**HOBBIES & INTERESTS:** *Clayton* — Music, Dancing, and Video Games; *Lisa* — Working with Children, Shopping, Cooking, Taking Care of Clayton

**FAVORITE TYPE OF MUSIC:** *Clayton* — Rap; Rhythm and Blues; Soul; *Lisa* — Rhythm and Blues; Soul

**FAVORITE SPORTS HERO:** *Clayton* — Walter Payton; *Lisa* — Magic Johnson

**FAVORITE TV/MOVIE STAR:** *Clayton* — Martin Lawrence and Eddie Murphy; *Lisa* — Martin Lawrence

**FAVORITE FOOD:** *Clayton* — New York Strip Steak; *Lisa* — Chicken Parmesan

**CHILDREN & AGES:** Dominique (Clayton's Son) — 5 yrs.; Expecting Their First Child in January of 1993

## HERSHEY-CHOCOLATE CAKE
## WITH CREAM CHEESE ICING

1 stick butter or margarine   1 c. self-rising flour
1 c. sugar   1/2 t. vanilla
4 eggs
1 large can Hershey Chocolate Syrup


Cream butter and sugar together. Add eggs, one at a time. Add remaining ingredients; mix well. Pour into pan (9" x 13"). Bake at 350 degrees for 45 minutes.

*Icing:* *      1 pkg. cream cheese (8-oz.)
           1 stick margarine
           1 box powdered sugar
           1 t. vanilla

Mix until smooth. Frost cake.

*\* Optional: Cake can be served cool with icing, or served warm by itself or with ice cream.*


## HOLMES' BROCCOLI CASSEROLE

2 pkgs. frozen broccoli (10-oz. pkg.)
1/2 c. mayonnaise
1 can mushroom soup (or cream of chicken soup)
1 onion, chopped
1 egg, beaten           3 c. bread crumbs
1-1/2 c. Cheddar cheese, shredded

Cook broccoli as directed on package; drain. Mix all ingredients in bowl; reserve some bread crumbs to spread on top. Pour into 9" x 11" x 2" pan; place bread crumbs on top. Bake at 350 degrees for 20 minutes. Serves 15-20 people. *(Optional: White chicken pieces can be added to dish before baking.)*

Clayton and Lisa Holmes on April 26, 1992 -- Draft Day

Clayton with his son, Dominique - 5 years old

## MANEESHA & ROBERT LEE JONES
### * *Number 55* *
### Linebacker — 6-2 — 238

BIRTHDATES: *Robert* — 9-27-69 (Blackstone, Virginia); *Maneesha* — 7-2-72 — (York, Pennsylvania)

COLLEGES: *Robert* — East Carolina University (Criminal Justice); *Maneesha* — West Virginia University (Psychology)

YEARS IN PROFESSIONAL FOOTBALL: 1991 Draft Choice

GREATEST MOMENT IN SPORTS: Sacked Rypien of Redskins on Monday Night Football

GREATEST THRILL ABOUT BEING A PRO ATHLETE: Playing with All the Athletes He Has Admired as a Youngster

FAVORITE ACADEMIC SUBJECT: *Maneesha* — Psychology and Spanish

WIFE'S OCCUPATION: Housewife — Taking Care of Rob

HONOR OR AWARDS: *Robert* — Unanimous All-America for Four Years; Finalist of Dick Butkus Award; Participant in East-West Shrine Game; MVP of Peach Bowl (1991 ECU vs. NC State); First-Round Draft Pick out of ECU; Honor Roll at ECU; *Maneesha* — Honor Roll in High School; Dean's List in College

FAVORITE AUTHOR: *Robert* — Alex Haley; *Maneesha* — Steven Spielberg

FAVORITE TYPE OF MUSIC: *Robert* — Rap and Reggae; *Maneesha* — Reggae; Rhythm and Blues; Native American

FAVORITE SPORTS HERO: *Robert* — Roger Staubach; *Maneesha* — Husband Robert

FAVORITE TV/MOVIE STAR: *Robert* — Dolomite (Rudy Ray Moore); *Maneesha* — Eddie Murphy and Martin Lawrence

FAVORITE FOOD: *Robert* — Southern Cooking; *Maneesha* — Shrimp

PET PEEVE: *Robert* — News Reporters Who Insult You and Still Ask for Interviews!

WORST FEAR: *Robert* — Sustaining a Permanent Injury

CHILDREN & AGES: Expecting First Child in April, 1993

Robert and Maneesha enjoying a night out together as newlyweds

The Jones' wedding day: July 4, 1992

## ROBERT JONES' "DIRT" DESSERT

Oreo cookies (32 oz.)                1/2 c. sugar
2 small vanilla pudding packages     1 stick butter
3 c. milk
carton of Cool Whip (12-oz.)
pkg. cream cheese (8-oz.)

Mix pudding and milk together; chill until it thickens. Add Cool Whip. In separate bowl, mix cream cheese, sugar, and butter on low speed. Combine pudding mixture into cream cheese mixture by spooning. In a large bowl or baking dish, layer cookies and pudding mixture (cookies first). Top with crushed cookies.

## MANEESHA'S ITALIAN SHELL CASSEROLE

1 lb. ground beef or Italian sausage  1 t. garlic salt
favorite spaghetti sauce (large jar)  1 t. oregano
1 c. onion, chopped                   1-1/2 t. black pepper
1 c. green pepper, chopped            1 t. crushed red pepper
Mozarella cheese, shredded (16 oz.)   Parmesan cheese
jumbo shells, cooked and drained
parsley

Brown meat, onion, and green pepper; drain. Season spaghetti sauce (garlic, oregano, and pepper); pour enough sauce in baking dish (9" x 13") to cover the bottom. Fill shells with meat mixture. Place shells, open side down, closely together. Cover shells with remaining sauce; top with Mozarella, Parmesan cheese, and parsley. Cover casserole with aluminum foil. Bake for 30-45 minutes. Makes 4-8 servings. *Serve hot and enjoy!*

## TODD JONES
*Newly-Acquired Player*
Guard -- 6-3 -- 295


**BIRTHDATE:** 7-3-67 (Hope, Arkansas)

**COLLEGE:** Henderson State College

**YEARS IN PROFESSIONAL FOOTBALL:** Orlando of the World League - 1 spring; Cleveland - 1991 Draft Choice; Dallas Cowboys - 1st Season

**HONORS OR AWARDS:** Small College All-America Honors in 1990

## TODD'S CORN-JALAPENO CASSEROLE

1 c. regular rice, uncooked
1 medium onion, chopped
1 medium green pepper, chopped
1 c. celery, chopped
1/2 c. butter or margarine, melted
1 T. sugar
1 jalapeno pepper, finely-chopped (*use 2, if you want hotter*)
2 cans cream-style corn (17-oz. can)
1 c. mild Cheddar cheese, shredded (4 oz.)
cherry tomato halves, optional
green pepper rings, optional
fresh parsley sprigs, optional

Cook rice according to directions on the package; set aside. Saute onion, green pepper, and celery in butter until vegetables are tender. Combine rice, sauteed vegetables. Add next 4 ingredients to rice and vegetable mixture; stir well. Spoon mixture into a lightly-greased baking dish (12" x 8" x 2"). Bake at 350 degrees for 40-45 minutes. Garnish with cherry tomatoes, green pepper rings, and parsley, if desired. Makes 10 servings.

## TODD JONES' SPICED APPLE SLICES

3 large baking apples, cored, peeled, and thinly-sliced
6 T. butter or margarine, melted
3 t. all-purpose flour
4 T. brown sugar
3/4 t. ground cinnamon
3 T. lemon juice

Arrange apple slices in a lightly-greased baking dish (1-qt.). Combine remaining ingredients; pour over apple slices. Bake at 350 degrees for 20 minutes. Makes 6 servings.

# JIMMY SMITH
## *Number 6*
### Wide Receiver — 6-1 — 205

**BIRTHDATE:** 2-9-69 (Jackson, Mississippi)

**COLLEGE:** Jackson State University

**YEARS IN PROFESSIONAL FOOTBALL:** 1991 Draft Choice

**GREATEST MOMENT IN SPORTS:** Scoring First College Touchdown

**GREATEST THRILL ABOUT BEING A PRO ATHLETE:** The Pay

**HONORS OR AWARDS:** All-Conference Performer at Calloway High in Jackson; Earned National Player of the Week Honors at JSU; Earned Second-Team All-Southwestern Athletic Conference Honors and a Spot on the Senior Bowl Roster

**HOBBIES & INTERESTS:** Traveling and Fishing

**FAVORITE TYPE OF MUSIC:** Rap

**FAVORITE SPORTS HERO:** Magic Johnson

**FAVORITE TV/MOVIE STAR:** Jasmine Guy

**FAVORITE FOOD:** Rice-a-Roni

**PET PEEVE:** Know-It-Alls

**WORST FEAR:** Failure to Succeed

## JIMMY'S FOOLPROOF CORNBREAD

1 c. plain cornmeal
1/2 c. all-purpose flour
1 c. fresh buttermilk
1 egg
2 T. oil
2 T. sugar
2 t. baking powder
1/2 t. baking soda

Combine all ingredients; mix well. Pour in iron greased skillet. Bake at 450 degrees until brown.

## JIMMY SMITH'S BUTTERMILK PIE

5 eggs
2 c. sugar
2 T. flour
1 stick margarine
2 t. vanilla
1 c. buttermilk
1 prepared 9" one-crust pie shell

Beat eggs well. Add sugar, flour, margarine, vanilla, and buttermilk. Pour into *unbaked* pie shell. Bake at 375 degrees for 45-50 minutes. Makes 1 deep 10" pie, or 2 shallow 9" pies.

Jimmy in the 3rd Grade -- 8 years old

Smith -- All-Star Performer at Jackson State

# KEVIN REY SMITH
## * Number 26 *
### Cornerback -- 5-11 -- 177

BIRTHDATE: 4-7-70 (Orange, Texas)

COLLEGE: Texas A & M (Recreation, Parks, and Tourism)

YEARS IN PROFESSIONAL FOOTBALL: 1991 Draft Choice

HONORS OR AWARDS: Earned Second-Team All-State Honors While Leading the West Orange Stark High School Team to a 15-0 Record and a Second Consecutive Texas 4-A State Championship; Big Part of Aggies Squad That Compiled a 27-3-1 Record, Including 1991 SWC Title; Played in Three Bowl Games during Football Career; Scored Six Special Teams/Defensive Touchdowns in Four Years at Texas A & M, Making Big Plays When Given the Opportunity; Set a SWC Record for Career Interceptions with 20, Tied the Conference Mark for Career Touchdowns on Interceptions with 3, and Set Texas A & M Career Records for Interceptions Yards (289) and Passes Defensed (32); Started 38 Straight Games to End Collegiate Career; Cornerstone of an Aggies' Secondary Named the Best in the Country by "The Sporting News" Prior to the Season, with the Aggies Leading the Nation in Defense and Finishing Second in the Country in Pass Defense in 1991; Semifinalist for Jim Thorpe Award, Given to the Nation's Best Defensive Back; Earned Consensus All-America Honors in 1991; for the Third Straight Year, All-SWC Recognition in 1991; Played in Japan Bowl and East-West Shire Game following Senior Year; in 1990, Earned SWC Defensive Player of the Week Mention; Picked Off Nine Passes -- the Second Most in a Season in Texas A & M History -- to Lead the SWC, and Finish Fourth in the Nation; 17th Overall Pick in 1992 Draft, Selected with the Highest Choice Ever Used on a Defensive Back from Texas A & M; First Aggie Player Drafted by Dallas since 1985; only the First Defensive Back Selected in the First Round by Dallas -- Chosen with the Highest Pick the Cowboys Have Ever Used on a Defensive Back; Has Uncanny Knack for Finding the Ball -- 4.5 Speed and Big Play Ability

Kevin Smith -- top Cowboy pick from Texas A & M, has an uncanny knack for finding the ball

Smith -- #1 Draft Choice in 1992 -- 4.5 speed and big play ability

## KEVIN'S SHRIMP-FILLED AVOCADOS

1/2 c. vegetable oil
1/2 c. lemon or lime juice
2 T. vinegar
2 t. capers
1-1/2 t. salt
1/2 t. dill seeds
1/2 t. dry mustard
dash of ground red pepper
1 lb. fresh medium shrimp, cooked, peeled, and deveined
3-4 ripe avocados

Combine first 8 ingredients in a large bowl; stir in shrimp. Cover; marinate overnight in the refrigerator. Drain shrimp; reserving marinade. Cut avocados in half lengthwise; remove seed, and peel. Brush avocados with reserved marinade; fill with shrimp mixture. Makes 6-8 servings.

## KEVIN SMITH'S POTATO BAKE

8 slices bacon, diced
4 T. onion, chopped
4 medium baking potatoes, cut into 1/4" slices
1/2 t. salt
1/4 t. pepper
1 c. whipping cream
1/2 c. chicken broth

Cook bacon and onion in a heavy skillet until bacon is crisp; drain well on paper towels. Set aside. Place potatoes in a lightly-greased baking dish (1-qt.); sprinkle with salt and pepper. Add whipping cream and broth. Top with bacon and onions. Cover; bake at 350 degrees for 45 minutes, until tender. Makes 4 servings.

# FALLON WACASEY
## * *Number 89* *
### Tight End -- 6-7 -- 241

BIRTHDATE: 2-8-69 (Billings, Montana)

COLLEGE: University of Tulsa (B.A. -- Communications)

YEARS IN PROFESSIONAL FOOTBALL: 1991 Draft Choice

GREATEST MOMENT IN SPORTS: Had Three Touchdowns during a High School Football Game

GREATEST THRILL ABOUT BEING A PRO ATHLETE: Thrill of Being around Some of the Greatest Athletes in the World

FAVORITE ACADEMIC SUBJECT: Marketing

HONORS OR AWARDS: Spring, 1992, Dean's Honor Roll; All-Academic Student-Athlete Honor Roll (1989-1992); Three-Time All-Conference Pick in Basketball in High School; Earned All-State Honors, as a Senior -- Averaging 24 Points and 14.3 Rebounds to Lead Team to the State 2-A Semifinal; All-America Honors as a Tight End in High School; Golden Hurricanes' Lineman of the Week; Selected with the Highest NFL Draft Choice Ever Used on a Tight End from Tulsa

HOBBIES & INTERESTS: Motorcycling, Fishing, and Spring Breaks on the Beach

FAVORITE AUTHOR: Stephen King

FAVORITE TYPE OF MUSIC: Rock 'n Roll

FAVORITE SPORTS HERO: Walter Payton

RAVORITE TV/MOVIE STAR: Sam Elliot

FAVORITE FOOD: Surf and Turf

PET PEEVE: Smokers and Bad Drivers

WORST FEAR: "Dancing with the Devil in the Pale Moonlight!"

## WACASEY'S EASY LASAGNA

| | |
|---|---|
| 2 lbs. ground beef | 1 t. salt |
| 3-1/2 c. spaghetti sauce | 1/4 t. pepper |
| 1-1/2 c. water | Lasagna, uncooked (8 oz.) |

2 c. Ricotta, or small curd cottage cheese (15 oz.)
3 c. Mozzarella, or Monterey Jack cheese, shredded (12 oz.)
1/2 c. Parmesan cheese, grated
2 eggs
1/4 c. parsley, chopped (optional)

Brown beef. Add sauce and water; simmer for 10 minutes (*will be watery, but that's okay*). Combine remaining ingredients, except Lasagna. Layer in pan, beginning with meat, Lasagna, meat, cheese, Lasagna, cheese, ending with meat. Cover with foil; bake at 350 degrees for 50 minutes. Remove foil; bake 10 minutes (uncovered). *Soooooo good!*

## FALLON'S TOMATOES AND GREEN BEANS

2 cans whole green beans, drained (16-oz. can)

| | |
|---|---|
| 4 cubes beef bouillon | 1 large onion, chopped in big |
| 1 can tomatoes | pieces |
| 1/4 t. black pepper | 1 c. water |

Mix all ingredients in pan. Bring to boil; simmer for 20 minutes. *Very tasty!*

## FALLON WACASEY'S PIG-LICKING CAKE

1 box pudding-style yellow cake mix
4 eggs
1/2 c. oil
1 can Mandarin oranges (11-oz.)
Cool Whip (9 oz.)
1 pkg. instant pudding mix (3-oz.)
1 large can crushed pineapple, drained

Preheat oven to 350 degrees. Mix together box pudding-style yellow cake mix, eggs, oil, and Mandarin oranges (for 2 min.). Pour mixture into 3 round cake pans. Bake for 20 minutes; remove from oven. Let cool. Mix instant pudding mix with Cool Whip. Add drained pineapple. Frost cake (*just the top*) with this mixture. *Very easy . . . and wonderful!*

208

Wacasey, pictured with his greatest fans -- his nieces and nephews: Carolyn, Colleen, Sam, Coy, Meagan, and Dillon

Fallon and his three sisters: Dede, Luiann, and Kim

# DARREN WOODSON
### * Number 28 *
Safety -- 6-1 -- 215

BIRTHDATE: 4-25-69 (Phoenix, Arizona)

COLLEGE: Arizona State University

YEARS IN PROFESSIONAL FOOTBALL: 1991 Draft Choice

GREATEST MOMENT IN SPORTS: Winning Junior High Basketball Championship in Eighth Grade

GREATEST THRILL ABOUT BEING A PRO ATHLETE: Traveling and Meeting New People

FAVORITE ACADEMIC SUBJECT: Math

HONORS OR AWARDS: Star Running Back at Maryvale High School, Helping Lead Team to the Semifinals of the AAA-1 Playoffs; Earned Honorable Mention All-Conference Honors, as a Sophomore, at ASU; Senior Captain of Team

HOBBIES & INTERESTS: Water Skiing, Basketball, Hanging out with Friends and Family

FAVORITE TYPE OF MUSIC: Rhythm and Blues

FAVORITE SPORTS HERO: Walter Payton

FAVORITE TV/MOVIE STAR: Bill Cosby

FAVORITE FOOD: "Anything Mom Cooks"

PET PEEVE: Dirty House

WORST FEAR: Not Being Able to Spend Time with Family, or Being Hurt and Not Being Able to Play Football

Darren Woodson -- one of the nation's hardest hitting players in 1991

Darren, a tremendous raw talent, will make the switch from linebacker to safety

## DARREN'S WESTERN BEANS

1-2 lbs. ground chuck
1 onion, minced
1 green pepper, minced
1/4 c. dill pickle
1/2 c. tomato juice
3 small cans pork and beans
2 t. Worcestershire sauce
1/2 c. barbecue sauce
2 T. mustard
2 T. brown sugar

Brown the ground chuck. Add onion, pepper, dill pickle, and tomatoe juice; cook until simmering. Add beans, Worcestershire sauce, barbeque sauce, mustard, and brown sugar. *The longer this simmers, the more flavorful it becomes.*

## WOODSON'S GREEN CHILI CASSEROLE

1-1/2 lb. ground beef
1 can cream of mushroom soup
1 can Cheddar cheese soup
1 small can green chilis
1 small can pimentos
1 pkg. taco tortilla chips
6 T. mild enchilada sauce
1 medium onion
1 T. chili powder

Brown ground beef; add onions. Slowly add chili powder; mix well. Put one-half of meat mixture in a baking dish. Layer one-half serving of remaining ingredients; repeat process, starting with the remaining meat and ending with cheese soup. Bake at 350 degrees, just long enough to heat thoroughly. Arrange whole taco chips around the edge of the dish before serving.

# COACHING STAFF

## GLORIA & HUBBARD LINDSEY ALEXANDER
### Assistant Coach
### Wide Receivers

**BIRTHDATES:** *Hubbard "Axe"* — 2-14-39 (North Carolina); *Gloria* — (None Given)

**COLLEGES:** *Axe* — Tennessee State; *Gloria* — Tennessee State (Education)

**GREATEST MOMENT IN SPORTS:** When University of Miami Won the National Championship

**WIFE'S OCCUPATION:** Teacher (Second Grade)

**HONORS OR AWARDS:** Axe — Earned All-America Honors at Center at Tennessee State and Signed as a Free Agent with Dallas; Began Coaching Career with His Alma Mater in 1962; after Seven Seasons as a Very Successful High School Coach in Memphis, Tennessee, Spent Six Seasons as an Assistant at Vanderbilt; Coached Ten Seasons at the University of Miami

**HOBBIES & INTERESTS:** *Gloria* — Decorating and Teaching

**FAVORITE AUTHOR:** *Gloria* — Tom DePaola

**FAVORITE TYPE OF MUSIC:** *Axe* — Rhythm and Blues; *Gloria* — Oldies

**FAVORITE TV/MOVIE STAR:** *Axe* — ESPN Sports Shows; *Gloria* — Erkle (from "Family Matters")

**FAVORITE FOOD:** *Axe* — Fish; *Gloria* — Mexican

**HOW THEY MET:** Met in College

**CHILDREN:** Todd, Chad, and Brad

214

Gloria and Axe met at Tennessee State

Hubbard's receiving unit stepped to the center stage of the offense with an exciting blend of younger players and proven veterans

## AXE'S SHRIMP CREOLE

3 lbs. shrimp, peeled
8 T. butter (1 stick)
8 T. flour
1 can tomato sauce (14-16 oz.)
2 c. onions, chopped
1 c. celery, chopped
1 c. green pepper, chopped
1 T. garlic, chopped
1 c. green onions, chopped
1 c. parsley, chopped
1 T. thyme
3 bay leaves
3 c. shrimp stock, or water with fish bouillon

1 T. basil
1 T. brown sugar
4 thin slices lemon
salt, to taste
cayenne pepper, to taste
cooked rice

Saute the shrimp in butter for 2-3 minutes; remove shrimp. To the butter, add the flour; stir over medium heat until lightly browned. Add the onions, celery, green pepper, and garlic. Saute the vegetables until they begin to turn transparent. Add the stock, tomato sauce, thyme, bay leaves, basil, brown sugar, lemon slices, salt, and pepper. Simmer for about 15 minutes. Add green onions, parsley, and shrimp the last 5 minutes of cooking. Serve over rice (cooked according to the directions on the package). Serves 8 people.

## GLORIA'S CLASSIC AMBROSIA

2 c. oranges (with juice), sliced
1/2 c. shredded coconut (fresh, if possible)
1/2 c. blanched almonds, chopped

Place orange slices in medium bowl. Sprinkle with coconut and almonds. Chill well before serving.

216

## JANE & NEILL ARMSTRONG
### Assistant Coach
### Coach (Retired)

BIRTHDATES: *Neill* – 3-9-26 (Tishomingo, Oklahoma); *Jane* – 4-11-25 (Neosho, Missouri)

COLLEGES: *Neill* – Oklahoma State University (B.S.); *Jane* –Oklahoma State University

PROFESSIONAL FOOTBALL OR COACHING EXPERIENCE: Played with Philadelphia Eagles (1947-1951); Canadian Football (1952-1954); Coached Oklahoma State University (1955-1961) and Houston Oilers (1962-1963); Head Coach in Edmonton, Canada (1964-1969); Coached Minnesota Vikings (1969-1977); Head Coach of Chicago Bears (1978-1981); Been with Dallas Cowboys (1982-1990)

HONORS OR AWARDS: Football All-America Honors; President of Student Association

HOW THEY MET: Met on Campus of Oklahoma A & M in 1943; Married in June, 1946

CHILDREN: Neill, Jr.; David; Gail; and Five Grandchildren

217

Neill and Jane Armstrong at home in Roanoke, Texas

## NEILL'S GRAPE ICE CREAM

6 whole eggs
1 c. sugar
juice of 1 lemon
2 cans Welch's frozen grape juice concentrate (12-oz. can)

Use one-gallon ice cream freezer. Beat eggs with beater until light and frothy. Add sugar, lemon juice, grape juice; blend well. Pour into freezer can; fill to mark with milk of your choice (half-and-half cream, homogenized milk, or a mixture of the above). Freeze according to freezer directions.

*We make this recipe with skim milk . . . and think the outcome is delicious!*

## JANE'S MOST SIMPLE CORNBREAD

1/2 c. flour
1/2 c. yellow cornmeal
3 t. baking powder
1/4 c. sugar
1 egg
1 T. oil
1/2 c. milk

Measure the dry ingredients together. Beat egg, oil, and milk together. Add dry ingredients to liquid mixture. Pour into heavy iron skillet (9"), which has been heated with approximately 1 T. of oil. Bake at 425 degrees for about 20 minutes. This method makes a very crispy bottom crust. May also be baked in *well-greased* muffin tins, cake pan, cornstick pan, etc. Easy to double the amount.

## DIANN & JOSEPH (JOE) W. AVEZZANO
### Assistant Coach
### Special Teams

BIRTHDATES: *Joe* -- 11-17-43 (Yonkers, New York); *Diann* -- 3-10-49 (Story City, Iowa)

COLLEGES: *Joe* -- Florida State (Major: Criminology); *Diann* -- Patricia Stevens (Fashion Merchandising)

GREATEST MOMENT IN SPORTS: National Championship, University of Pittsburgh

FAVORITE ACADEMIC SUBJECT: *Joe* -- Math; *Joyce* -- English

WIFE'S OCCUPATION: Wholesale Jewelry Business

HONORS OR AWARDS: *Joe* -- President of Student Body; Named NFL Special Teams Coach of the Year in 1991 by the Widest Margin Ever; *Joyce* -- Female Lead in High School Musical All Four Years; Sang Professionally While Living in Pittsburgh

FAVORITE TYPE OF MUSIC: *Joe* -- Country (Like All Types); *Joyce* -- Like All Music

FAVORITE SPORTS HERO: *Joe* -- "None -- I Respect Athletic Personalities; Heroes Are Reserved for Everyday People and Family"

FAVORITE FOOD: *Joe* -- Italian Foods (Especially Rigatoni); *Joyce* -- Sushi

HOW THEY MET: Met While Joe Was Coaching at Iowa State University; on His Lunch Hour, Came into the Clothing Store Where Joyce Worked (Her Hometown -- Ten Miles from Iowa State University in Ames)

CHILDREN & AGES: Tony - 16 yrs.

220

Joe, with wife, Diann, has made a visible impression around the league in only his second year as an NFL coach

Tony Avezzano, age 16, doing what he does best . . . EATING

## JOE'S MOM'S "SECRET" MEATBALL
## AND PORK SPAGHETTI

*Meatballs:*

| | |
|---|---|
| 1 to 1-1/2 lbs. ground beef | salt and pepper, to taste |
| 2-3 eggs | garlic powder, to taste |
| 3-4 pieces dried bread, soaked in water | |
| 1/2 c. Parmesan cheese | pork ribs, or Italian sausage |

Mix all ingredients (except for ribs or sausage) with hands. Form into balls; fry in olive oil. In same pan, fry boneless pork ribs, or good sweet Italian sausage.

*In separate pot, simmer:*

> 3 cans tomatoes, crushed (28-oz. can)
> garlic powder, to taste
> black pepper, coarse-ground
> oregano
> 3-4 whole bay leaves
> salt

After frying the meatballs and pork (or Italian sausage), put them into the tomato sauce mixture. Do not drain grease from the frying pan. Add a *large can of tomato paste* to grease in frying pan, plus some water to thin; simmer this, making a tomato gravy. After all browning from pan has cooked into paste, pour into pan of crushed tomatoes and sauce. Simmer at least 3 hours (*the longer, the better*). Serve over any pasta. Makes 4-5 meals.

*\*This is a huge amount -- you may freeze what's left.*

### JEAN WALKER'S SWEET POTATOES

| | |
|---|---|
| 3-4 c. sweet potatoes, mashed | vanilla |
| 1/2 c. sugar | pinch of salt |
| 1/2 c. milk | |

Mix the ingredients; put in casserole.

| *Topping:* | 1 c. brown sugar | 1/3 c. flour |
|---|---|---|
| | 1/2 stick margarine | 1/2 c. milk |
| | 1 c. nuts (pecans are best) | |

Mix the ingredients; pour over potatoes. Bake at 350 degrees for 25-30 minutes.

222

## DIANA & ROBERT BLACKWELL

### Video Director

BIRTHDATES: *Robert* – 12-1-50 (Dallas, Texas); *Diana* – 5-25-58 (Louisville, Kentucky)

COLLEGES: *Robert* – Stephen F. Austin State University (B.S. – Communications); *Diana* – Moorpark Junior College

FAVORITE ACADEMIC SUBJECT: *Robert* – Photography; *Diana* – Math

WIFE'S OCCUPATION: Flight Attendant

HONORS OR AWARDS: *Robert* – Most Witty; *Diana* – Most Likely to Succeed

FAVORITE AUTHOR: *Robert* – Mark Twain; *Diana* – John Grisham

FAVORITE TYPE OF MUSIC: *Robert and Diana* – Little Bit of Everything

FAVORITE SPORTS HERO: *Diana* – Michael Jordan

FAVORITE TV/MOVIE STAR: *Diana* – Richard Gere

FAVORITE FOOD: *Robert* – Lasagna; *Diana* – Mexican

WHERE THEY MET: Met Each Other in 1983 When Diana Was Working on the American Airlines Team Charter to Washington

PET PEEVE: *Robert* – People Who Don't Do Their Best

CHILDREN & AGES: Nathan Rivers - 5 yrs.

## ROBERT'S FRESH APPLE COOKIES

| | |
|---|---|
| 1/2 c. shortening | 1/8 t. salt |
| 1-1/3 c. brown sugar, firmly-packed | 1 t. ground cinnamon |
| | 1/2 t. ground nutmeg |
| 1 egg | 1/2 t. ground cardamon |
| 1/4 c. milk | 1 c. raisins |
| 2 c. all-purpose flour | 1 c. pecans, chopped |
| 1 t. baking soda | 1 c. unpeeled apples, finely-chopped |

Cream shortening; gradually add sugar, beating well. Add egg and milk; beat well. Combine flour, soda, salt, and spices; add to creamed mixture, mixing well. Stir in raisins, pecans, and apples. Drop dough by teaspoonfuls onto greased cookie sheet. Bake at 400 degrees for 12-15 minutes. Cool on wire rack; frost with vanilla frosting.

*Vanilla Frosting:*  1-1/2 c. powdered sugar, sifted
1/8 t. salt  2-1/2 T. milk
1 T. butter or margarine, melted
1/2 t. vanilla extract

Combine all ingredients in a small mixing bowl. Beat until smooth. Yields 4-1/2 dozen cookies.

## DIANA'S "SHOW STOPPER" BEAN DISH

| | |
|---|---|
| 2 pkg. frozen green peas | 1 pkg. frozen lima beans |
| 2 pkg. frozen French-cut green beans | mayonnaise |
| Parmesan cheese (3 oz.) | small carton whipping cream |

Cook vegetables separately, according to directions on the packages; drain well (*very important*). Mix beans. Fold in mayonnaise and whipping cream. Place in rectangular baking dish. Sprinkle Parmesan cheese over top. Bake at 350-375 degrees until bubbly and cheese is brown. If too dry, add a little milk while baking.

The Blackwells at home in Coppell, Texas, with son, Nathan

Diana, who is a flight attendant, holding Nathan - 5 years old

## JOYCE & JOSEPH (JOE) BRODSKY
### Assistant Coach
### Running Backs

BIRTHDATES: *Joe* -- 6-9-34 (Miami, Florida); *Joyce* -- "Birthday - Yuk!" (Brooklyn, New York)

COLLEGES: *Joe* -- University of Florida (B.S. and Masters in Administration and Supervision); *Joyce* -- University of Florida and University of Miami (B.A. -- Education)

GREATEST MOMENT IN SPORTS: Winning State Football Championship with Son, Joe, as Quarterback

GREATEST THRILL ABOUT BEING A PRO COACH: Being around Great Athletes and Good People

FAVORITE ACADEMIC SUBJECT: *Joe* -- Archeology; *Joyce* -- English Literature

WIFE'S OCCUPATION: Retired School Teacher

HONORS OR AWARDS: *Joe* -- Four-year Letterman in Football, Basketball, and Track at Florida; for 13 Seasons, One of South Florida's Most Successful High School Coaches; Won State Football Championship While Coaching High School; Had First Team in the State to Go 14-0; While Coaching Running Backs at University of Miami for 11 Seasons, Won Two National Championships; *Joyce* -- Graduated *Cum Laude* from University of Miami; Valedictorian of Senior Class

HOBBIES & INTERESTS: *Joe* -- Golf, Fishing, and Family; *Joyce* -- Taking Care of Grandchildren (Amanda - 5 yrs.; and Joey - 2 yrs.); Reading, All Sports, and Singing

FAVORITE AUTHOR: *Joyce* -- James Michener and Leon Uris

FAVORITE TYPE OF MUSIC: *Joe* -- Country Western and Classical; *Joyce* -- Pop, Country, and Classical

FAVORITE SPORTS HERO: *Joe* -- His High School Basketball Coach, Joe McNulty; *Joyce* -- Larry Brodsky

FAVORITE TV/MOVIE STAR: *Joe* -- John Wayne and Three Stooges; *Joyce* -- Dustin Hoffman and Paul Newman

FAVORITE FOOD: *Joe* -- Lobster and Stone Crabs; *Joyce* -- Rack of Lamb and Rice Pilaf

CHILDREN & AGES: Joe, Jr. - 34 yrs. (Wife: Robin; and Two Grandchildren: Amanda and Joey); Larry - 31 yrs.; and Jeffrey - 30 yrs. (Wife: Francis)

226

Amanda & Joe, Jr. (top left); Robin & Joey (top right); Joyce & Joe (center); Francis, Jeffrey, & Joe (bottom left); & Larry (bottom right)

## JOE'S STANDING PRIME RIB ROAST

prime rib roast, small end
fresh garlic
potatoes (optional)
black pepper, freshly-ground
dry mustard (Colman's)
paprika

Preheat oven to 500 degrees. Stuff as many fresh garlic pieces into the roast as you can (*the more, the better*). Sprinkle freshly-ground black pepper all over the roast. Generously cover roast with dry mustard, patting with fingers. Cover lightly with paprika for color. Place meat *standing* in roasting pan in 500-degree oven; brown for 20-25 minutes. Turn oven down to 350 degrees; cook for approximately 22 minutes per pound, for medium rare. Remove; let stand (covered) for 15 minutes for easy slicing. Can add small potatoes in pan; let them cook in the juices while the roast is baking (for last 45 minutes).

*Joe's mother, Lee, gave us this recipe.*

### JOYCE'S GARBANZO BEAN SALAD

1 can Progresso garbanzo beans
2 onions, sliced
1/2 c. olive oil
2 T. fresh lemon juice
paprika

1 T. wine vinegar
salt
6-7 Greek olives
(optional)

Drain garbanzo beans; rinse well with cool water. Place beans in flat pie dish (8"). Slice (*do not chop*) onions as thinly as possible. Place onions in bowl, pouring a lot of salt over them; mix well. Cover; let sit for 15-20 minutes. Mix olive oil, lemon juice, and vinegar in cup; add dash of salt. Mix (*may add a bit more lemon juice*). Rinse onions in cool water well, removing *all* salt and squeezing onions -- making them limp and removing *all* liquid. Spread onions over garbanzo beans, covering beans completely. Sprinkle salt lightly over the onions. Pour olive-oil mixture slowly over all of the beans. If possible, tip pie dish and remove olive-oil mixture into cup; then pour same mixture again over the beans. Sprinkle lightly with paprika for color. Place olives on top. Cover and refrigerate. Serve cool anytime. Serves 4 people. *This goes great with rice dishes, lamb, or flank steak.*

*Joyce's mother, Vicky, gave us this recipe.*

228

# GERALDINE & WILLIAM T. (BUCK) BUCHANAN

## Equipment Manager

BIRTHDATES: *Buck* – 5-24-33 (Ballinger, Texas); *Geraldine* – 7-20-37 (Rockingham, North Carolina)

COLLEGE: *Buck* – Angelo State College

GREATEST MOMENT IN SPORTS: With the Cowboys, When They Won Super Bowl XII against the Denver Broncos

FAVORITE ACADEMIC SUBJECT: *Buck* – Math; *Geraldine* – English

WIFE'S OCCUPATION: Grandmother, Inc.

HONORS OR AWARDS: *Buck* – Spending Twenty Years in the Military, Awarded the Bronze Star Medal for His Performance during a Tour in Takhli, RTAFB, Thailand, from 1968 to 1969; Returned to the U.S. Air Force Academy, Remaining There until Retiring in 1973

HOBBIES & INTERESTS: *Buck* – "Honey Do" Projects Everywhere; *Geraldine* – House Renovation; Three Grandsons – William T. Buchanan, II - 6 yrs.; Jonathan Brett Buchanan - 3 yrs.; and David Andrew Rodriguez - 4 yrs.

FAVORITE AUTHOR: *Buck* – Louis L'Amour; *Geraldine* – Danielle Steel

FAVORITE TYPE OF MUSIC: *Buck and Geraldine* – Oldies, but Goodies

FAVORITE SPORTS HERO: *Buck* – Enos "Country" Slaughter (St. Louis Cardinals - Baseball); *Geraldine* – Husband Buck

FAVORITE TV/MOVIE STAR: *Buck* – Sharon Stone; *Geraldine* – Tom Cruise

FAVORITE FOOD: *Buck* – Any and All Sweets; *Geraldine* – Chocolate / Vanilla Yogurt

CHILDREN & AGES: Julie Renee - 35 yrs.; William Andrew (Bucky) - 31 yrs.

## BUCK'S CHICKEN BREAST IN WINE SAUCE

6 chicken breasts, boneless
1 can cream of celery soup
1 can cream of chicken soup
1/2 c. sherry
Cheddar cheese, grated (6 oz.)
almonds, slivered
rice, cooked according to package directions

Put chicken breasts in baking dish. Mix together all other ingredients; pour over breasts. Bake at 275 degrees (uncovered) for 2-1/2 hours. Serve over rice. Serves 6 people.

## GERALDINE'S APPLE MUFFINS

1-1/4 c. oil
2 c. sugar
3 c. flour
3 eggs
2 t. vanilla
1 t. baking soda
1 t. salt
2 c. tart apples, peeled and cubed
1 c. pecans, chopped
1 c. coconut
1 t. cinnamon
1/4 c. raisins

Combine oil, eggs, and vanilla. Add remaining ingredients; stir until well-moistened. Grease muffin tins; fill until 2/3 full. Bake at 350 degrees for 25 minutes. Makes 3 dozen muffins.

Geraldine and Buck Buchanan at home in December, 1991

## KAY & DAVID (DAVE) CROSS CAMPO
### Assistant Coach
### Defensive Backs

BIRTHDATES: *Dave* -- 7-18-47 (New London: Connecticut); *Kay* -- 7-22-56 (Ogden, Utah)

COLLEGES: *Dave* -- Central Connecticut State University (B.S. -- Physical Education); Albany State University (M.S. -- Educational Communications); *Kay* -- Stevens Henager College

GREATEST MOMENT IN SPORTS: Winning the National Championship (1987) at the University of Miami

PROFESSIONAL COACHING EXPERIENCE: College Coaching -- 18 yrs.; Pro Coaching -- 4 yrs.

HONORS OR AWARDS: Twice Earned All-East Honors at Shortstop at Central Connecticut State

HOBBIES & INTERESTS: *Dave* -- Guitar, Music, and Golf; *Kay* -- Crafts

WIFE'S OCCUPATION: Homemaker and Mother

FAVORITE AUTHOR: *Dave* -- Tom Clancy; *Kay* -- Danielle Steel

FAVORITE TYPE OF MUSIC: *Dave* -- 50's Rock and Roll; *Kay* -- Country

FAVORITE SPORTS HERO: *Dave* -- Frank Gifford

FAVORITE TV/MOVIE STAR: *Dave* -- The Late Jackie Gleason; *Kay* -- Richard Gere

FAVORITE FOOD: *Dave* -- Italian; *Kay* -- Chinese

HOW THEY MET: Met in Ogden, Utah, While Dave Was Coaching at Weber State College

CHILDREN & AGES: Angie - 17 yrs.; Eric - 16 yrs.; Shelbie - 12 yrs.; and Michael - 1 yr. (Dave Also Has 2 Children in Connecticut: Becky -- 15 yrs.; and Tommy -- 13 yrs.

Kay and Dave Campo, who joined the Cowboys in 1989, after guiding the secondary at the University of Miami

The Campo children: Michael - 15 months; Eric - 16 years; Angie - 17 years; and Shelbie - 12 years

## DAVE'S GRANDMA CAMPO'S TOMATO SAUCE

1 large onion, finely-minced
1 clove garlic (optional)
1/4 t. salt
1 can tomato sauce (8-oz.)
1/4 t. cinnamon, or more to taste
1/4 t. nutmeg, or more to taste
1/4 t. cloves, or more to taste
1 green pepper, finely-minced
2-3 pork chops
1/8 t. black pepper
1 can tomatoes (14-oz.)
2 c. water
1 c. ketchup

Saute finely-minced onion and green pepper in a small amount of oil (garlic, if desired). Finely cube pork chops; brown with onions and peppers. Add remaining ingredients; simmer for 1-2 hours until thickened. Serve over pasta, polenta, or gnocchi.

### KAY'S CARAMEL BROWNIES

1 box German Chocolate Cake Mix
1/3 c. evaporated milk
3/4 c. melted butter
1 c. nuts, chopped
60 Kraft caramels

Mix cake mix, milk, butter, and nuts together. Spread 1/2 of mixture in 9" x 12" greased pan. Bake at 350 degrees for 4 minutes. Meanwhile, melt caramels with 1/2 c. evaporated milk. Remove brownies from oven; carefully spread caramel mixture over brownies. Top with remaining half of cake mixture. Continue to bake for another 18-20 minutes. Cool slightly; put in refrigerator for 30 minutes.

234

## JANET & DONALD RAY COCHREN
### Athletic Trainer
### Medical Records Coordinator

BIRTHDATES: *Don* -- 2-6-32 (Oakland City, Indiana); *Jan* -- 7-25-43 (Warrenton, Missouri)

COLLEGES: *Don* -- Purdue University (Physical Therapy); *Jan* -- Northeast Missouri State (Sociology and Psychology)

GREATEST MOMENT IN SPORTS: Winning Super Bowl VI

GREATEST THRILL ABOUT BEING A PRO ATHLETIC TRAINER: Working with High-Caliber Athletes

FAVORITE ACADEMIC SUBJECT: *Don* -- Biology; *Jan* -- Sociology and Psychology

WIFE'S OCCUPATION: Wife, Mother, and Homemaker

HONORS OR AWARDS: *Don* -- Earned Physical Therapy Certificate at Pennsylvania; Joining the Dallas Cowboys in 1965, Became Medical Records Coordinator / Athletic Trainer after Working 25 Seasons as the Team's Trainer; One of the 28 Trainers Selected from Colleges and Professional Sports Teams to Serve the United States Team at the 1980 Winter Olympics in Lake Placid, New York; in 1984, Received the 25-Yr. Honor Award from the National Athletic Trainers Association; in 1989, Chosen to Serve as a Member of the Professional Football Athletic Trainers/Gatorade Advisory Board; *Jan* -- Nominee for Volunteer of the Year

HOBBIES & INTERESTS: *Don* -- Jogging, Spending Time with Family, and Going to Chris' Games; *Jan* -- Working with People, Traveling, Volunteer Work, and Being with Family and Friends

FAVORITE AUTHOR: *Don* -- Sidney Sheldon; *Jan* -- Danielle Steel

FAVORITE TYPE OF MUSIC: *Don* -- Good Jazz and Country Western; *Jan* -- New Wave

FAVORITE SPORTS HERO: *Don* -- Stan Musial; *Jan* -- Babe Ruth

FAVORITE TV/MOVIE STAR: *Don* -- Andy Griffin and John Wayne; *Jan* -- Kirk Douglas, Michael Douglas, and Richard Gere

FAVORITE FOOD: *Don* -- Spaghetti; *Jan* -- Tex-Mex

CHILDREN: Jeff - 27 yrs.; Wendy - 26 yrs.; Scott - 25 yrs.; and Chris - 15 yrs. (WR and DB on Shepton High "A" Football Team)

## DON'S CHOLESTEROL-FREE BANANA BREAD

2-1/4 c. all-purpose flour
2/3 c. honey-crunch wheat germ
1/2 c. oats, uncooked
1/4 c. packed brown sugar
1 T. baking powder
1/2 t. salt
1/4 t. baking soda
10 T. light corn oil or margarine (1-1/4 sticks)

1-1/2 c. bananas, mashed (about 3 bananas)
1 can frozen apple juice concentrate, thawed (6-oz.)
1/2 c. frozen eggs substitute, thawed
1/3 c. walnuts, chopped
1 t. vanilla extract

Preheat oven to 350 degrees. Grease 9" x 5" loaf pan. In large bowl, mix first 7 ingredients. With pastry blender, cut in margarine until mixture resembles course crumbs. Stir in bananas, undiluted apple juice concentrate, egg substitute, walnuts, and vanilla, just until flour is moistened. Spoon batter into pan. Bake 60 minutes, or until toothpick inserted in center of bread comes out clean. Cool bread in pan on wire rack for 10 minutes; remove from pan and cool slightly. Serve warm, or cool completely to serve later.


## JAN'S MARINATED VEGETABLES

1/2 head cauliflower, cut into florets
3 large carrots, pared and cut into 2" strips
3 ribs celery (1" pieces)
1 can baby corn
1 green pepper, cut into strips
1 can button mushrooms, drained (8-oz.)
3/4 c. white wine vinegar
1/2 c. olive oil
2 T. sugar

1 t. salt
1/2 t. oregano
1/4 t. pepper
1 can pimento, drained, cut in strips (4-oz.)
1 can pitted black olives, drained (#303 can)
1 jar green pimento olives, drained
1 can artichoke hearts, cut in quarters
1/4 c. water
1 bottle low-calorie Italian dressing

Mix ingredients (except Italian dressing) together in Dutch oven; cover. Bring to a boil. Reduce heat; simmer for 5 minutes. Cool quickly. Add the low-calorie Italian dressing. Refrigerate (covered) 24 hours before serving. Keeps for 4-6 weeks in refrigerator (covered).

Chris Cochren -- 15 years old, a wide receiver and defensive back on Shepton High School "A" football team

Don and Jan Cochren on NFL Sports Cruise

# TAMMY & PAUL (BUTCH) HILTON DAVIS
## Assistant Coach
## Defensive Line

BIRTHDATES: *Butch* -- 11-17-51 (Tahlequah, Oklahoma); *Tammy* -- 2-3-61 (Wellington, Kansas)

COLLEGES: *Butch* -- University of Arkansas (B.S. -- Science); *Tammy* -- Florida Atlantic University (B.S. -- Business Administration)

GREATEST MOMENT IN SPORTS: 1987 National Championship and 1991 Playoff Win at Chicago

GREATEST THRILL ABOUT BEING A PRO COACH: Helping Players Reach Their Goals

FAVORITE ACADEMIC SUBJECT: *Butch* -- Anatomy and Physiology; *Tammy* -- Marketing

WIFE'S OCCUPATION: Systems Marketing Specialist (Xerox Corporation)

HOBBIES & INTERESTS: Butch -- Golf, Travel, Reading, and Water Sports; Tammy -- Golf, Dance, Water Sports, Snow Skiing, Reading, and Community Involvement Work; Serving Third Year as Chairperson for the Xerox Community Involvement Projects (XCIP) at Xerox at Infomart

FAVORITE AUTHOR: *Butch* -- Tom Clancy and James Michener; *Tammy* -- Norman Vincent Peale

FAVORITE TYPE OF MUSIC: *Butch and Tammy* -- All Types of Music

FAVORITE FOOD: *Butch* -- Steak or Mexican; *Tammy* -- Mexican

CHILDREN & AGES: Expecting First Child in February

Tammy and Butch make their home in Coppell, Texas

## BUTCH'S OKLAHOMA SPAGHETTI PIE

1 pkg. spaghetti (6-oz.)
2 T. butter or margarine
1/3 c. Parmesan cheese, grated
2 eggs, well-beaten
1 c. cottage cheese (8 oz.)
1 can tomatoes, chopped (8-oz. can, or 1 c.)
1 can tomato paste (6-oz.)
1 t. sugar
1 t. dried oregano, crushed
1/2 t. garlic salt
1/2 c. Mozzarella cheese, shredded (2 oz.)

1 lb. ground beef or pork sausage
1/2 c. onion, chopped
1/4 c. green pepper, chopped

Cook the spaghetti according to the package directions; drain. Stir butter or margarine into hot spaghetti. Stir in Parmesan cheese and eggs. Form spaghetti mixture into a "crust" in a buttered pie plate (10"). Spread cottage cheese over the bottom of the spaghetti crust. In a skillet, cook ground beef or pork sausage, onion, and green pepper until vegetables are tender and meat is browned; drain off excess fat. Stir in *undrained* tomatoes, tomato paste, sugar, oregano, and garlic salt; heat through. Place meat mixture into the spaghetti crust. Bake (uncovered) at 350 degrees for 20 minutes. Sprinkle Mozzarella cheese on top. Bake for 5 minutes longer, or until cheese melts. Makes 6 servings.

## TAMMY'S MARINATED VEGETABLE SALAD

3/4 c. vinegar
1/2 c. vegetable oil
1 t. salt
1/2 c. sugar
1 T. water
1 t. pepper
1 can French-style green beans, drained (16-oz.)
1 can small peas, drained (17-oz.)
1 can shoe peg whole kernel corn, drained (12-oz.)
1 jar pimentos, chopped and drained (2-oz.)
1 c. celery, chopped
1 green pepper, finely-chopped
1 bunch green onions, chopped

Combine first six ingredients in a medium saucepan; bring to a boil, stirring to dissolve sugar. Cool. Combine vegetables; stir in vinegar mixture. Cover; place in refrigerator for 12 hours, stirring occasionally. Approximately 8 servings.

*Dallas Cowboys Wives' Cookbook*

## JANICE & ROBERT L. FORD
### Assistant Coach
### Tight Ends

**BIRTHDATES:** *Robert* – 6-21-51 (Belton, Texas); *Janice* – 4-8-54 (Saginaw, Michigan)

**COLLEGES:** *Robert* – University of Houston (B.S. – Education) and Western Illinois University (M.A. – Athletic Administration

**GREATEST MOMENT IN SPORTS:** First 99-Yard Touchdown Pass

**FAVORITE ACADEMIC SUBJECT:** *Janice* – History

**WIFE'S OCCUPATION:** Homemaker and Mother

**HONORS OR AWARDS:** *Robert* – Only Player in the History of the NCAA to Catch Two 99-Yd. Touchdown Passes; Led Houston in Receiving, Punt Returns, and Kickoff Returns in 1972, Earning Third-Team All-America Honors; College Hall of Fame Finalist

**HOBBIES & INTERESTS:** *Robert* – Golf and Bowling; *Janice* – Bowling, Tennis, Golf, and Reading

**FAVORITE AUTHOR:** *Robert* – John Grisham; *Janice* – Sidney Sheldon and Danielle Steel

**FAVORITE TYPE OF MUSIC:** *Robert* – Pop (Soft); *Janice* – "Good" Jazz

**FAVORITE SPORTS HERO:** *Robert* – Paul Warfield; *Janice* – Jim Thorpe and Nolan Ryan

**FAVORITE TV/MOVIE STAR:** *Robert* – Robert Wagner; *Janice* – Kevin Costner and Dustin Hoffman

**FAVORITE FOOD:** *Robert* – Chicken Fried Steak and Mashed Potatoes; *Janice* – Mexican or Italian (Depending on What Day It Is)

**PET PEEVE:** *Robert* – Snobbish People

**WORST FEAR:** *Robert* – Being Surrounded by Snakes

**CHILDREN & AGES:** Bobby - 16 yrs. (Senior, Coppell High); and Jason - 14 yrs. (Starting QB and MLB, Coppell High)

241

## ROBERT FORD'S BAKED PASTA

2 T. olive oil
1 lb. lean ground beef
3 cloves garlic, peeled and crushed
1/2 c. half and half
3/4 c. marinara or spaghetti sauce
3/4 c. brown gravy *(homemade is best, but from a jar is okay)*
1/4 c. Parmesan cheese
1 t. oregano
1/2 t. rosemary
salt and pepper, to taste
3/4 lb. Penne pasta *(short, small tubes)*

Bring 4 qts. water to a boil. Brown the meat and garlic in olive oil; drain excess fat. Add all remaining ingredients, except the cheese (for topping) and the pasta. Simmer while your pasta cooks, until it is just slightly tender. Drain pasta; mix with meat sauce. Top with cheese. Bake in a 3-qt. pan at 350 degrees for 25 minutes (uncovered).

## JANICE'S BAKED STRAWBERRY CUSTARD

4 eggs
2-1/3 c. milk
1/2 c. sugar
1/2 t. almond extract
1/4 t. salt
2 c. fresh (sliced) or frozen unsweetened strawberries
cinnamon (optional)
whipping cream, whipped

In a medium bowl, beat eggs; blend in milk, sugar, almond extract, and salt. Stir in 1-1/2 c. of strawberries. Place 6-oz. custard cups in a 9" x 13" pan on oven rack. Divide custard mixture evenly *(cups should be almost full)*; sprinkle with cinnamon. Pour boiling water into pan around custard cups *(about 1" deep)*. Bake at 325 degrees for 50-60 minutes. Chill; top with whipped cream and remaining strawberries.

Janice and Robert Ford in Western attire, going to the rodeo

Jason Ford -- 14 years; and Bobby Ford -- 16 years

# RAFFAELLA (RAFFY) & STEVE HOFFMAN
## Assistant Coach
### Kickers/Quality Control

**BIRTHDATES:** *Steve* -- 9-8-58 (Camden, New Jersey); *Raffaella (Raffy)* -- 9-23-66 (Vimercate, Italy)

**COLLEGES:** *Steve* -- Dickinson College (B.A. -- Economics; and St. Thomas University (M.A. -- Sports Administration); *Raffy* -- Oxford Institute of Languages (Monza, Italy)

**GREATEST MOMENT IN SPORTS:** Dallas Cowboys' Playoff Win vs. Chicago

**GREATEST THRILL ABOUT BEING A PRO COACH:** Every Game Day in the NFL

**FAVORITE ACADEMIC SUBJECT:** *Steve* -- Economics, Italian; *Raffy* -- Foreign Languages

**WIFE'S OCCUPATION:** International Flight Attendant

**HONORS OR AWARDS:** *Steve* -- All-Mid-Atlantic Conference Honors in Football in 1978 and 1979; All-Mid-Atlantic Conference Honors in Baseball in 1979 and 1980

**HOBBIES & INTERESTS:** *Steve* -- Enjoys Staying in Shape, Listening to All Types of Music, and Studying Italian

**FAVORITE AUTHOR:** *Steve* -- Leon Uris; *Raffy* -- Alberto Bevilacqua, Fra Leslo Alberoni

**FAVORITE TYPE OF MUSIC:** *Steve* -- "Anything But Joe Avezzano Singing Country or Dave Campo Singing Bee-Bop"; *Raffy* -- Club Music

**FAVORITE SPORTS HERO:** *Steve* -- Ed Podolak; *Raffy* -- Fabio Del Medico (Italian Soccer Player)

**FAVORITE TV/MOVIE STAR:** *Steve* -- Robert DiNero; *Raffy* -- Kevin Costner

**FAVORITE FOOD:** *Steve* -- Pasta (*"Anyway You Can Make It"*); *Raffy* -- Pasta!

**PET PEEVE:** *Steve* -- Unsalted, Overcooked Pasta Served at So-Called "Great" Italian Restaurants

**WORST FEAR:** *Steve* -- Sleeping through My Alarm and Missing an Important Staff Meeting

Steve met his wife, Raffy, who is an international flight attendant, while coaching in Italy

## STEVE'S SPAGHETTI WITH CLAM SAUCE

2 cans whole baby clams (10-oz. can)
6-7 cloves of fresh garlic, chopped
2/3 c. parsley, chopped
1/3 c. olive oil — white table wine
1 can crushed tomatoes (8-oz.) — Parmesan cheese

In a small saucepan, lightly saute garlic in olive oil over a low-medium heat. Add half of the chopped parsley; add clams (drained). Simmer for 8-10 minutes; add tomatoes. Add rest of parsley; cook for 15-20 minutes over low-medium heat. If you like, you can add 1/4 to 1/2 c. white table wine; *let it evaporate as sauce cooks.* Pour sauce over 1 lb. cooked spaghetti; stir in Parmesan cheese, to taste. Serve. Makes 4-5 servings.

*Pasta "Al Dente" (for all pasta dishes):*

Boil 3 qts. of water in a large pot. Add 2 T. salt to water. Add about 1 lb. of pasta of your choice (*spaghetti is best for the clam sauce*). Read the cooking directions on the package. If the directions call for a cooking time of 9-12 minutes, cook it for 9 minutes and *no longer. Always cook to the lower end of the time scale on the package!*

## RAFFY'S RISOTTO MILANESE

1 lb. of *your favorite* rice — 3 T. butter
2 pkgs. saffron (or capsules) — 3 T. olive oil
1/2 medium onion, chopped — 1 c. dry white wine
3 cloves garlic, chopped — chicken broth
2 strips of bacon, chopped — sprinkle of nutmeg
1/2 c. mushrooms (*dried are best*), chopped
salt, pepper, and Parmesan cheese (*as you please*)

Into a 4-qt. pot, melt butter into the olive oil. Add chopped onions and garlic; saute until both are a very light gold color (*don't let them brown!*). Add chopped bacon strips and mushrooms; cook until mushrooms are tender. Add rice; stir until the rice is coated. Add a couple of ladles of chicken broth (which is being kept hot in another saucepan). Stir frequently while cooking; cook until broth is absorbed. Continue to add a couple ladles of broth at a time, cooking off the broth each time before adding more. Continue this process until rice is tender and is the consistency of a thick rice pudding (*make sure the rice doesn't stick to the pan!*). Add saffron, wine, plenty of Parmesan cheese, a sprinkle of nutmeg, and salt and pepper, to taste. Ready to serve as a main dish or as a side dish with fish or meat.

## ROSANNE & JIM MAURER

### Assistant Trainer

BIRTHDATES: *Jim* -- 3-8-65 (Dallas, Texas); *Rosanne* -- 2-23-65 (Dallas, Texas)

COLLEGES: *Jim* -- Southern Methodist University (B.A. -- Physical Education; University of North Texas (Working on M.A. in Physical Education); *Rosanne* -- Texas Tech

GREATEST MOMENT IN SPORTS: First Playoff Victory at Chicago in 1991

GREATEST THRILL ABOUT BEING A PRO TRAINER: Watching an Athlete Overcome an Injury and Then Come Back to Perform at His Best Again

FAVORITE ACADEMIC SUBJECT: *Jim* -- History

WIFE'S OCCUPATION: Housewife and Mommy

HONORS OR AWARDS: *Jim* -- National Honor Society in High School

HOBBIES & INTERESTS: *Jim* -- Golf and Racquetball

FAVORITE AUTHOR: *Rosanne* -- Emmett Fox

FAVORITE TYPE OF MUSIC: *Jim* -- Bruce Springstein; *Rosanne* -- All Kinds of Music

FAVORITE SPORTS HERO: *Jim* -- Walter Payton

FAVORITE TV/MOVIE STAR: *Jim* -- Alan Alda; *Rosanne* -- Cher

FAVORITE FOOD: *Jim* -- Barbecue Ribs (Tony Romas); *Rosanne* -- Italian (All Kinds!)

PET PEEVE: *Jim* -- Players Who Sit at My Desk and Go through My Things (You Know Who You Are!)

WORST FEAR: *Jim* -- Snakes

CHILDREN & AGES: Nicholas Paul -- 3-1/2 yrs.; Benjamin Michael -- 3-1/2 mon.

## JIM MAURER'S ARTICHOKE
## AND GREEN BEAN CASSEROLE

1/2 c. onion, chopped
2 cloves garlic
1/2 c. olive oil
Progresso Italian-Style Bread Crumbs
2 cans artichoke hearts
2 cans green beans, drained

Saute onion and garlic in olive oil until soft. Add artichoke hearts, green beans, and Progresso Italian-Style Bread Crumbs to sauteed ingredients. Cook for 5 minutes in skillet. Remove from stove. Spray Pam on casserole dish; place all ingredients in dish. Sprinkle additional Progresso Italian-Style Bread Crumbs on top. Bake at 350 degrees for 20-25 minutes.


## ROSANNE'S SHRIMP SCAMPI ITALIANO

1 c. Wishbone Robusto Herbal Italian Dressing
1 lb. uncooked shrimp, cleaned and deveined

In a large, shallow broiler pan, pour dressing over shrimp. Cover; marinate in refrigerator, turning occasionally, for at least 2 hours. Broil shrimp with dressing, turning shrimp and basting with dressing until done. Makes 4 servings.

Roseanne and Jim were married on December 7, 1991, and live in Dallas

"Little" Cowboy Nicholas enjoys playing with Dad, while Benjamin looks on

# KATHRYN (KATHY) & BRUCE B. MAYS

## Director of Football Operations

BIRTHDATES: *Bruce* — 8-16-43 (Cleveland, Ohio); *Kathryn Miller (Kathy)* — 1-6-48 (Detroit Michigan)

COLLEGES: *Bruce* — Ohio Northern University (B.S. — Education); The University of Akron (M.S. — Education); Oklahoma State University (Course Work Completed for Doctorate in Higher Education); *Kathy* — Oklahoma State University (B.S. and M.S.)

GREATEST MOMENT IN SPORTS: Winning National Championship in Miami in 1987

FAVORITE ACADEMIC SUBJECT: *Bruce* — Management; *Kathy* — Nutrition

WIFE'S OCCUPATION: Registered Dietitian at Cooper Clinic - Cooper Aerobic Center

HOBBIES & INTERESTS: *Bruce* — Read, Golf, and Running

FAVORITE AUTHOR: *Bruce* — Ernest Hemingway; *Kathy* — Margaret Mitchell

FAVORITE TYPE OF MUSIC: *Bruce* — Symphony; *Kathy* — Classical Piano

FAVORITE SPORTS HERO: *Bruce* — Otto Gragham; *Kathy* — Michael Irvin

FAVORITE TV/MOVIE STAR: *Bruce* — John Wayne; *Kathy* — Harrison Ford

FAVORITE FOOD: *Bruce* — Italian and Chinese; *Kathy* — Bagels, Apples, Pasta, and Chinese

HOW THEY MET: Met in Stillwater, Oklahoma, Where Bruce Was Assistant Athletic Director, Working on His Doctorate, and Kathy Was Working on Her Masters

PET PEEVE: *Bruce* — Leaving the Lights on

CHILDREN & AGES: Kirsten - 23 yrs.; Jennifer - 17 yrs.; Laura - 14 yrs.; and Damien - 14 yrs.

Bruce and Kathy Mays, who is a registered dietitian at Cooper Clinic/Cooper Aerobic Center

The Mays' daughters: Kirsten - 23 years; and Jennifer - 17 years

## BRUCE'S BEIROX

1/2 recipe "Rolls"
1-1/2 lb. hamburger
1/3 head cabbage, shredded
1 onion, chopped
1/2 green pepper, chopped
cooking oil

Brown hamburger, crumbling fine as it cooks; drain and cool. Saute shredded cabbage, onion, and pepper with a tablespoon or so of oil until tender; drain and cool. Season both fairly liberally. Mix together. (*Some kids only want hamburger in theirs, so you can leave some plain.*) Roll dough on floured board until about 1/3" thick; cut in squares about 5" x 5". Place a large spoonful of meat mixture in the center. (*If meat is hot, the bread will rise a little and Beirox will be a little doughy.*) Fold four corners to center; close seams by pinching dough together. Place seam side down on cookie sheet. Bake at 400 degrees until lightly browned.

*Rolls:*

2 pkg. yeast                          1/2 c. shortening
4 c. lukewarm water            1 T. salt
1 c. sugar

Add 8-10 c. flour, or more, until dough forms a ball. Knead lightly. Place in oiled bowl; cover with Saran Wrap. Refrigerate. Take out the amount needed (*the rest will keep for a week or so*).

## KATHY'S HOLIDAY AMBROSIA

1 can pineapple chunks (20-oz.)
2 cans Mandarin orange segments (11-oz. can)
1-1/2 c. seedless red grapes
2 large red delicious apples, cut up in chunks
1/2 pkg. miniature marshmallows
1 c. flaked coconut
1/2 c. nuts
2 c. vanilla yogurt (add more as needed)

Drain pineapple and oranges. Combine pineapple, oranges, grapes, apples, marshmallows, coconut, and nuts. Stir yogurt into fruit mixture. Chill. Serves 8-10 people.

## ANNE & KEVIN P. O'NEILL

### Head Athletic Trainer

BIRTHDATE: *Kevin* -- 8-2-54 (Pittsburgh, Pennsylvania); *Anne* -- 12-26-?? (Los Angeles, California)

COLLEGE: *Kevin* -- University of Pittsburgh (B.S. -- Physical Education); University of Arizona (M.S. -- Athletic Training; *Anne* -- Oregon State University (B.S. -- Home Economics)

GREATEST MOMENT IN SPORTS: Winning the National Championship at the University of Miami

FAVORITE ACADEMIC SUBJECT: *Kevin* -- English; Sports Psychology; *Anne* -- Art History; European History

WIFE'S OCCUPATION: Program Coordinator for the U.S.D.A. Childcare Food Program; Employed by Southwest Human Development Services of Austin, Texas

HONORS OR AWARDS: *Anne* -- High School Senior Class President

HOBBIES & INTERESTS: *Kevin* -- Jogging, Water Skiing, and Spending Time with Daughters; *Anne* -- Reading, Exercising, Crafts, Love of Water and Water Sports

FAVORITE AUTHOR: *Kevin* -- John Grisham and Leon Uris; *Anne* -- Danielle Steel

FAVORITE TYPE OF MUSIC: *Kevin* -- All Different Types; *Anne* -- Jazz and Classical

FAVORITE SPORTS HERO: *Kevin* -- Roberto Clemente; *Anne* -- Mary Decker-Slaney

FAVORITE TV/MOVIE STAR: *Kevin* -- Clint Eastwood; *Anne* -- Katharine Hepburn

FAVORITE FOOD: *Kevin* -- Coconut Creme Pie; *Anne* -- Chocolate

HOW THEY MET: Met in Corvallis, Oregon, in 1982, through a Mutual Friend; Married July 23, 1983

CHILDREN & AGES: McKenzie - 7 yrs. (a gymnast); and Kaitlyn - 6 yrs. (into Acting and Voice Classes)

## O'NEILL'S PITTSBURGH ACINI DE PEPI SOUP

1 chicken fryer
3 chicken bouillon cubes
1 large onion, diced
1/3 lb. *acini de pepi* noodles, cooked and drained
2-1/2 t. salt
1 t. rosemary
3 bay leaves
1 t. sugar
1 t. parsley

Put chicken in pot; add water (2" over chicken). Add all ingredients (except noodles). Cook at medium heat for 1-1/2 hours. Remove chicken; debone. Cook with chicken pieces until boiling. Add dumpling mixture (a teaspoon at a time); put in *acini de pipi* noodles.

*Dumpling Mixture*:   2 eggs, beaten
2/3 c. Romano cheese
1 T. flour

### ANNE'S OREGON BLACKBERRY COBBLER

1/4 c. butter
1/2 c. sugar
1 c. flour
2 t. baking powder
1/2 c. milk
4 c. Oregon blackberries
1 c. liquid (remaining juice and water)

Cream butter and sugar together. Sift flour and baking powder together; add milk. Mix altogether to make soft batter. Spread batter into bottom of pan (7" x 11"). Mix berries, sugar, and liquid together. Pour over batter. Bake at 350 degrees until done (30-35 minutes).

O'Neill Family: McKenzie, Neill, Anne, and Kaitlyn

Kevin, Anne, and daughters, Kaitlyn and McKenzie, relaxing by the family pool

## CAROL & BOB SLOWIK
Assistant Coach /
Defensive Assistant

BIRTHDATES: *Bob* -- 5-16-54 (Pittsburgh, Pennsylvania); *Carol* -- 12-4-54 (Fort Meade, Maryland)

COLLEGES: *Bob* -- University of Delaware (Masters - Education); *Carol* -- University of Delaware (B.A. - Liberal Studies)

GREATEST THRILL ABOUT BEING A PRO COACH: Being with a Team Like the Cowboys

FAVORITE ACADEMIC SUBJECT: *Bob* -- Science; *Carol* -- Teaching Classes

WIFE'S OCCUPATION: Homemaker; Teacher by Trade

HONORS OR AWARDS: *Bob* -- As a Two-Year Starter, Helped the Fighting Blue Hens to a Two-Year Record of 16-6, including the Quarterfinals of the NCAA Division 1-AA Playoffs, as a Senior; in 1991, Coached Outside Linebackers for a East Carolina University Team That Garnered Its Highest National Ranking (Ninth), the Best Record (11-1) in School History, and Its First winning Season and Bowl Appearance since 1983; *Carol* -- Track and Field Competitor on International Teams and Championship Teams

HOBBIES & INTERESTS: *Bob* -- Golf and Other Outdoor Sports; *Carol* -- Most Interests Outdoor-Related

FAVORITE TYPE OF MUSIC: *Bob and Carol* -- All Types

FAVORITE SPORTS HERO: *Carol* -- Chris Everett

FAVORITE TV/MOVIE STAR: *Bob* -- Clint Eastwood

FAVORITE FOOD: *Bob* -- Pizza and Pasta; *Carol* -- Pasta and Fish

HOW THEY MET: Met in College; Married in College

CHILDREN & AGES: Ryan - 11 yrs.; Andrea - 9 yrs.; Bobby - 5 yrs.; and Steven - 3-1/2 yrs.

Bob Slowik is the latest addition to the Cowboys' coaching staff

The Slowik Family: Andrea - 9 years; Carol; Bobby - 5 years; Bob; Steven - 3-1/2 years; Ryan - 11 years

## BOB'S UNIVERSITY OF FLORIDA
## CRAB MEAT CASSEROLE

2 cans crab meat
1 can whole tomatoes
1 carton sour cream (16-oz.)
1 onion, chopped
1 green pepper, chopped
2 t. butter
1 c. Cheddar cheese
spaghetti

Saute chopped onion and green pepper in butter. Mix with crab meat, tomatoes, sour cream, and 1/2 c. cheese. Cook spaghetti according to directions on the package; drain. Mix all ingredients together in casserole; top with remaining 1/2 c. cheese. Bake at 350 degrees for 30-40 minutes. Serves 4 people.


## CAROL'S NORTH CAROLINA PECAN TARTS

*Crust:*         1 pkg. cream cheese (3-oz.)
                1 stick margarine
                1 c. flour

Mix and break into small balls (the size of a walnut); mold into tiny-size muffin pans. Bake at 375 degrees for 15 minutes.


*Filling:*       1 egg
                1 t. vanilla
                3/4 c. brown sugar
                1 c. pecans, finely-chopped

Mix and spoon 1 T. of mixture into each shell. Sprinkle a few more ground pecans on top. Bake at 325 degrees for 10 minutes.

# NANCY & NORVAL (NORV) TURNER
## Assistant Coach
### Offensive Coordinator/Quarterbacks

BIRTHDATES: *Norv* -- 5-17-52 (Camp Le Jeune, North Carolina); *Nancy* -- 7-11-52 (Pasadena, California)

COLLEGES: *Norv* -- University of Oregon (B.S. - History); *Nancy* -- San Diego State University (B.S. - Child Development)

PROFESSIONAL COACHING EXPERIENCE: Nine Years Assistant at U.S.C.; Six Years with Los Angeles Rams; and Second Year with Dallas Cowboys

WIFE'S OCCUPATION: Housewife

HOBBIES & INTERESTS: *Norv* -- Barbecuing, Golf, and Family; *Nancy* -- Tole Painting, Children, and Football

FAVORITE AUTHOR: *Nancy* -- John Steinbeck and Sidney Sheldon

FAVORITE TYPE OF MUSIC: *Norv* -- Country Western

FAVORITE TV/MOVIE STAR: *Norv* -- Tom Whitenight and Jack Nicholson; *Nancy* -- Tom Whitenight and Kevin Costner

FAVORITE FOOD: *Norv* -- Italian; *Nancy* -- Mexican

HOW THEY MET: Norv, an Assistant Coach at U.S.C., and Nancy, the Head Coach's Secretary, When They First Met

CHILDREN & AGES: Scott - 10 yrs.; Stephanie - 8 yrs.; and Drew - 3 yrs.

## NANCY'S CALIFORNIA POPPY SEED SALAD

1 head Romaine lettuce
1 pt. fresh strawberries, sliced
1 Bermuda (red) onion, sliced

| *Dressing:* | 1/2 c. mayonnaise | 1/4 c. whole milk |
|---|---|---|
| | 2 T. vinegar | 2 T. poppy seeds |
| | 1/3 c. sugar | |

Place in jar, cover, and shake until blended. This will keep in the refrigerator for several days.

*\*Great summer salad!*

## NORV'S OSSOBUCO

1/2 c. all-purpose flour, unsifted
1-1/2 t. salt
1/2 t. pepper, freshly-ground
8 veal shanks, 1-1/2" thick (5 lbs.)
1/4 c. olive oil, approximately
2 large carrots, pared and cut crosswise into 1/2" pieces
2 large celery stalks, cut crosswise into 1" pieces
1 large onion, cut into wedges
2 large cloves garlic, crushed
1 can plum tomatoes, drained with seeds removed (28-oz.)
1-1/2 c. dry white wine
1 can chicken broth (14-oz.)
3/4 t. dried basil leaves, crushed
1/2 t. dried thyme leaves, crushed
1/2 lb. fresh spinach leaves, washed

On sheet of waxed paper, combine flour, 1 t. salt, and pepper. Coat veal shanks with flour mixture. In Dutch oven, heat 2 T. oil over medium heat. Brown shanks, a few at a time, on all sides (about 10 minutes each batch), adding oil as necessary, and removing shanks as they brown. In hot drippings in pan, saute carrots, celery, onion, and garlic for 8 minutes. Stir in tomatoes, wine, chicken broth, basil, thyme, and 1/2 t. salt, breaking up tomatoes. Bring to boiling; add shanks. Simmer (covered) for 50 minutes, or until veal is tender. With slotted spoon, remove shanks and vegetables to serving platter; keep warm. Over high heat, boil liquid in pan until reduced by half (about 10 minutes). Add spinach; over medium heat, cook for 3 minutes, or until tender. Pour spinach and liquid in pan over shanks.

*\*Note: If you are not serving the Ossobuco immediately, wait until reheating the dish to add fresh spinach.*

Turner Family: Norv, Stephanie, Drew, Scott, and Nancy

Drew - 3 years; Stephanie - 8 years; and Scott - 10 years

## JAN & DAVID (DAVE) RAYMOND WANNSTEDT
### Assistant Head Coach
### Defensive Coordinator/Linebackers

**BIRTHDATES:** *Dave* – 5-21-52 (Pittsburgh, Pennsylvania); *Jan* – 12-29-52 (Pittsburgh, Pennsylvania)

**COLLEGES:** *Dave* – University of Pittsburgh (B.S. – Physical Education; M.S. – Curriculum and Supervision); *Jan* – Robert Morris/Golden West College (Inst. for the Deaf – Deaf Students)

**GREATEST MOMENT IN SPORTS:** National Championship at University of Miami

**GREATEST THRILL ABOUT BEING A PRO ATHLETE:** Having Positive Influence on Society

**FAVORITE ACADEMIC SUBJECT:** *Dave* – Psychology; *Jan* – Sociology

**WIFE'S OCCUPATION:** Housewife

**HONORS OR AWARDS:** *Dave* – Offensive Tackle at Pittsburgh from 1970-1973, Earned Second-Team All-East Honors; Captain on the 1973 Panthers Team; Team Captain of 1973 Fiesta Bowl Team; Inducted into the Western Pennsylvania Sports Hall of Fame

**HOBBIES & INTERESTS:** *Dave* – Jogging and Golf; *Jan* – Golf and Reading

**FAVORITE AUTHOR:** *Dave* – Alan Mobley; *Jan* – Sidney Sheldon

**FAVORITE TYPE OF MUSIC:** *Dave* – Mix; *Jan* – Jazz and Country

**FAVORITE TV/MOVIE STAR:** *Jan* – Billy Crystal

**FAVORITE FOOD:** *Dave and Jan* – Italian

**HOW THEY MET:** Met in High School; Started to Date at Age 15

**CHILDREN & AGES:** Keri - 15 yrs.; and Jami - 12 yrs.

Dave Wannstedt is pictured with his wife, Jan, and daughters, Jami and Keri

Wannstedt cheerleaders: Jami - 12 years; and Keri - 15 years

## DAVE'S GRILLED FLANK STEAK

3/4 c. oil
1/4 c. soy sauce
3 T. honey
2 t. red wine vinegar
1 clove garlic, crushed
1-1/2 t. ground ginger
1 green onion, chopped
1 flank steak

Combine all ingredients, except steak. Pour over steak in large plastic bag in shallow pan. Let stand in refrigerator about 5 hours, turning several times. Grill about 2" above coals to desired doneness on each side. Slice steak diagonally, across grain. Serves 4 people.

## JAN'S ARTICHOKES AND CHEESE

2 cans artichokes, water-packed (8-1/2 oz. can)
1 stick butter, melted
3/4 c. flour
milk
1/2 t. Worcestershire sauce
1/4 t. paprika
dash of red and black pepper
1/2 lb. Cheddar cheese, grated

Drain artichokes; save liquid. Place liquid in saucepan; add melted butter. Add flour. Stir in enough milk to make a medium white sauce. Add Worcestershire sauce, paprika, and peppers. Add half the grated cheese; cook until melted. Place artichokes in a 2-qt. baking dish. Pour cheese mixture over artichokes. Sprinkle the remaining cheese over artichokes. Bake at 325 degrees for 45 minutes. Makes 6 servings.

# ANTHONY (TONY) CHARLES WISE
## Assistant Coach
## Offensive Line

BIRTHDATE: 12-28-51 (Albany, New York)

COLLEGE: Ithaca College (B.S. — Physical Education); University of Bridgeport, Conn. (M.A. — Education)

GREATEST MOMENT IN SPORTS: Winning 1987 National Championship at Miami

FAVORITE ACADEMIC SUBJECT: Exercise Physiology

HONORS OR AWARDS: Lettered in Football, Lacrosse, and Hockey at Ithaca College; Began Coaching Career at Albany State in 1973; Served Stints at Central Connecticut State, Washington State, University of Pittsburgh, Oklahoma State, Syracuse University, and University of Miami; in 1989, His First Year with Dallas, the Offensive Line Allowed Only 30 Sacks in 16 Games -- Tying the Team Record from 1976, When the NFL Schedule Was Just 14 Games

HOBBIES & INTERESTS: Jogging, Travel, and Mountain Hiking

FAVORITE TYPE OF MUSIC: Oldies (50's and 70's)

FAVORITE SPORTS HERO: Mickey Mantle

FAVORITE TV/MOVIE STAR: Robert DeNiro

FAVORITE FOOD: Italian

Tony Wise has shaped an offensive line that led Emmitt to two consecutive Pro Bowl appearances & an NFL lead in rushing in 1991

One of Wise's main interests is mountain hiking

## WISE'S NOODLE PUDDING

1 lb. broad noodles, drained and rinsed
1 pt. sour cream
1 lb. cottage cheese
1 c. milk
2-1/2 t. salt
4 T. sugar
6 T. margarine, melted
Kellogg's Cornflake Crumbs

Cook noodles according to directions on package; drain. Rinse with cold water (in a colander). Mix noodles with sour cream, cottage cheese, milk, salt, sugar, and margarine; place in shallow, greased casserole dish. Top with Kellogg's Cornflake Crumbs. Dot with lots of margarine (*use Fleishman's Corn Oil Margarine*). Refrigerate for a few hours or overnight. Remove from refrigeration; bring to room temperature. Bake at 375 degrees for 1-1/2 hours. Makes 12 servings.

## TONY'S SPINACH CASSEROLE

1 c. mayonnaise
1 can cream of celery soup
onion, minced or grated (in a jar)
3 pkgs. frozen spinach
1 c. sharp cheese
Kellogg Cornflake Crumbs

Mix mayonnaise with cream of celery soup. Add some minced or grated onion (in a jar). Cook frozen spinach; drain in colander. Mix in mayonnaise/soup mixture. Place in baking dish. Top with grated sharp cheese and Kellogg Cornflake Crumbs. Bake at 350 degrees for 1/2 hour.

## MIKE WOICIK
### Assistant Coach
### Strength and Conditioning

BIRTHDATE: 9-26-56 (Westwood, Massachusetts)

COLLEGE: Boston College (B.A. -- History); Springfield College (M.A. -- Physical Education)

HONORS OR AWARDS: Outstanding Discus Thrower at Boston College, Setting a School Record of 180' 5"; Earned All-East Honors and Qualified for the NCAA Championships; Came to Dallas after Serving Ten Years as the Strength and Conditioning Coach at Syracuse University

HOBBIES & INTERESTS: Bowling, CD Collecting, and Golf

FAVORITE AUTHOR: Robert Ludlum

FAVORITE TV/MOVIE STAR: John Wayne

FAVORITE FOOD: Prime Rib

Under Mike Woicik's leadership, the Cowboys entered 1991 in arguably the best physical shape ever

The conditioning program Woicik established helped the Cowboys through one of its most injury-free seasons in 1991

## MIKE'S DATE STICKS

*Mixture #1:*  1 pkg. dates, cut-up finely (2-oz.)
1 c. water
1 c. sugar

Boil ingredients until thick; let stand.

*Mixture #2:*  1 c. butter, melted        2 c. flour
1 c. brown sugar         2 c. oatmeal
1 t. soda

Mix Mixture #1 together. Put one-half of Mixture #2 in a 9" x 13" pan. Then put all of Mixture #1 on top. Cover with the other half of Mixture #2. Bake at 325 degrees for 30 minutes. Cool; cut in squares to serve.

## MIKE WOICIK'S SALMON BALLS

1 can fancy salmon                 1/2 t. horseradish
cream cheese, softened (8 oz.)     dash Tabasco
1/4 t. liquid smoke                2 T. onion, grated
1/4 t. salt                        1 T. lemon juice

Combine all ingredients. Form in ball shape. Chill. Serve with rice crackers.

## WOICIK'S COFFEE CAKE

1/2 c. butter                  2 c. flour
1 c. sugar                     1/2 t. salt
2 eggs                         1 t. baking powder
1 t. vanilla                   1 t. baking soda
1 c. sour cream

Cream butter, sugar, and eggs for 10 minutes; add vanilla. Sift dry ingredients together; add to creamed mixture, alternating with sour cream. Pour one-half batter in greased tube (angel food) cake pan. Spread one-half filling on the batter. Pour in rest of batter. Sprinkle remaining filling on top. Bake at 350 degrees for 45 minutes.

*Filling:*  1/2 c. nuts, chopped
1/4 c. brown sugar
2 t. cinnamon

Mix together well.

270

*Dallas Cowboys Wives' Cookbook*

# RECIPE INDEX

271

Page

| | Page |
|---|---|
| Patt Evans' Crunchy Jumbles | 182 |
| Robert Blackwell's Fresh Apple Cookies | 224 |

### *ITALIAN DISHES*

| | |
|---|---|
| Butch's Oklahoma Spaghetti Pie | 240 |
| Dave's Grandma Campo's Tomato Sauce | 234 |
| Jason's Linguine and Creamy White Clam Sauce | 188 |
| Joe's Mom's "Secret" Meatball and Pork Spaghetti | 222 |
| Leslie's Apple-to-Round Pizza | 71 |
| Lin's Chicken Spaghetti | 176 |
| Maneesha's Italian Shell Casserole | 198 |
| Marla's Sun-Dried Tomato Pesto | 147 |
| Patt's Pasta Primavera | 182 |
| Raffy's Risotto Milanese | 246 |
| Robert Ford's Baked Pasta | 242 |
| Rosanne's Shrimp Scampi Italiano | 248 |
| Steve's Spaghetti with Clam Sauce | 246 |
| Wacasey's Easy Lasagna | 208 |

### *MEAT DISHES*

| | |
|---|---|
| Aikman's Black Buck Trail Drive Style | 19 |
| Johnston's Herbed Butterflied Leg of Lamb | 83 |
| Norv's Ossobuco | 260 |

#### *(Beef Dishes)*

| | |
|---|---|
| Bruce's Beirox | 252 |
| Dave Wannstedt's Grilled Flank Steak | 264 |
| Evonne Hill's Roast Beef | 63 |
| Jerry's and Gene's Chili Stuff | 5 |
| Joe Brodsky's Standing Prime Rib Roast | 228 |
| John's San Francisco Bruno | 47 |
| Russell's Aunt Delores' Barbecue Short Ribs | 99 |
| Tony Casillas' Stew | 35 |

#### *(Chicken & Poultry Dishes)*

| | |
|---|---|
| Alfredo's Miami Marinated Mango Chicken | 119 |
| Alvin's Homemade Chicken Pot Pie | 55 |
| Angela's Granny's Chicken and Dumplings | 111 |
| Buck's Chicken Breast in Wine Sauce | 230 |
| Emmitt's Chicken Barbecue Sauce | 127 |
| Leon's Sunday Chicken and Rice | 91 |
| Russell's Chicken Breast Supreme | 99 |

273

*Dallas Cowboys Wives' Cookbook*

274

To order additional copies of the DALLAS COWBOYS WIVES' COOKBOOK (SECOND EDITION), simply fill out the convenient order form, clip, and mail to:

DALLAS COWBOYS WIVES' COOKBOOK (ED. II)
HAPPY HILL FARM ACADEMY/HOME
STAR ROUTE, BOX 56
GRANBURY, TEXAS 76048

Please Make Your Check or Money Order Payable to:
HAPPY HILL FARM

Please send _____ Cookbook(s) (Edition II) to:

Name _____

Address _____

City, State, Zip _____

Enclosed is a check or money order for **$12.95 for each Cookbook, plus $1.50 each for postage and handling.**

$ _____ Total Amount Enclosed

Please send _____ Cookbook(s) (Edition II) to:

Name _____

Address _____

City, State, Zip _____

Enclosed is a check or money order for **$12.95 for each Cookbook, plus $1.50 each for postage and handling.**

$ _____ Total Amount Enclosed

277